Random Thoughts of a Creative Mind

Random Thoughts of a Creative Mind

A life's journey of the creative process.

Sue Hassel

Random Thoughts of a Creative Mind
A Life's Journey of the Creative Process

Library of Congress Control Number: *2020903366*
ISBN-13: Paperback: *978-1-64749-065-2*

Inspirational/ Poetry

Printed in the United States of America

GoToPublish LLC
1-888-337-1724
www.gotopublish.com
info@gotopublish.com

Contents

Fourth of July

Fourth of July, 1993 New York City, not much to do. Elliot and I spent half the day in bed, the remainder stocking our shelves with food and goodies for our cat family; reruns of World War II footage as a point of reference, anticipating a rather boring evening at home. Then suddenly our TV prompts footage and onsite reporting of that evening's events, interviewing an entire family of Italians who have spent their lives making firecrackers, demonstrating how they are exploded, retelling stories of the good old days before the modern explosives were invented with an eye toward protecting anyone attempting detonating fire crackers.

Actually very interesting, since I never thought about it seriously, having grown up on a farm in the middle of Wisconsin, the closest we ever came was driving into Merrill on Highway 51 8 miles in the family car and then standing on a hill and looking down into the distance on 20 acres of farm land just north of Merrill.

Those days neighbors would pool together and pay someone in the southern states who drove into Illinois with a pickup truck loaded with fireworks. They were of course illegal. I remember going on a trip through eight states in two weeks (think a rural Ozzie and Harriet) – which was the normal length of the family vacation. Those days my father drove full time for an oil company delivering fuel locally during the days and then once home, milking 40 head of brown swiss cows (my dad's day started at 6 a.m. milking the same cows – at that hour he had a young assistant helping him). Those years echoed the hold over of farm help demonstrated by the Roosevelt years and the recovery from the great depression. Our hired man's name was John and he lived in one of our upstairs bedrooms, a nice kid who matured while becoming part of our immediate family. Eventually he left us to work in a factory in Merrill. Oh yes, the trip to Illinois for fireworks. I remember as a kid a two week car trip out west in which we visited 7 states checking out the state parks, visiting distant relatives. When we drove through Kentucky (we couldn't miss the stallion stations and the beautiful horses) we began to see fireworks for sale along the roadside. In Georgia the same. All over the place. So since my father was selling oil on the truck every day, he checked with his customers and found out that one of them routinely shipped firecrackers up to Wisconsin for July 4th, and a few phone calls later, we had a startup time and location for the July 4 festivities.

However, before the official July 4th fireworks north of Merrill, we had to put on our own family July 4th parade. My father, knowing horses well, and knowing how horses that were used to farm life would react to a noisy parade in Merrill with floats and bands and whatnot and a greenhorn rider ... thought it better that we put on our own family parade. And so we did, with a few cherry bombs and sparklers to begin (those fireworks were so miniscule that they were thought safe). Then we brought out Sporty (the family dog) who pulled a red wagon in which our very placid mother cat sat watching her kittens in the box on top. Of course audience interaction was encouraged complete with some snacks and viewers petting the kittens. Next was a pet sheep, Woolly, who very contentedly walked on lead and stopped in front of Grandma – if you chucked Woolly's chin he would wag his tail on cue. Then my sis, Bev and I came out with our horses, Judy (an appaloosa) and Silver (a palomino) all neatly groomed with full saddle packs and as much silver on them that the Montgomery Ward Catalog provided with the original saddles. After which there would be an outside treat of watermelon and ice cream sundaes under the trees near the house. Our little parade with prep and take down and snack took two hours, which left enough time to grab a quick nap before dusk overtook us.

The four of us piled into the pink Plymouth station wagon (Grandma did not go out at night) and drove into Merrill roughly 15 minutes away. Once at the city limits we checked the directions that daddy had from his customer which lead us 20 miles north of Merrill. I couldn't imagine anyone seeing fireworks in that desolate area, but we turned on to a dusty side road going two miles east and there was the hill. The closer we got the worse the parking got, and we parked our car to the side of the road and walked the rest of the way. About a 100 people had been tipped off to the activities – for Merrill – that was pretty good since there was no way to legally notify anyone. The legal fireworks – which were adequate but predictable - happened at the Fair Grounds.

The people had already claimed their places for the performance, men and women sitting on blankets from home. We stood in the back row. However, the mood of the crowd was good, only a few people brought beer and they were moderate in their drinking. The fireworks were generally more modest than those in the bigger cities, however it was far more exciting since the men detonating them were not sure where they would fly and they counted on the hill and distance to protect the attendees. There were a few good airborn flashes but nothing really prolonged. Finally the last rocket firework. It didn't leave a huge lit trail, but it whistled like crazy and then began to lose altitude and finally sputtered to the earth. The crowd began jeering. To save face the guys working the display had a backup plan and that one worked to the crowds pleasure. The actual finale was more effective since there was a row of continuous sparkling flashes ground level - all very visible – and the neighborhood quartet of musicians, i.e. trumpet, fiddle, accordian and trombone provided a loud if less than professional backdrop to the evening. On the way out you could buy a shorty beer (Pabst used to make a one serving size) and home-made rootbeer.

Oh yes, New York City 1993: Elliot and I decided to go to the Macy fireworks. We checked the subway connections to get there. Only one connection. We took the N to the Village and got off. The excitement was already building on the train. Not the usual bored preoccupied and vigilant New Yorkers going to work, but entire families with lots of kids. The train was packed everyone dressed for the occasion. Women in saris, Pakistani dress with trousers, Hispanics with very colorful skirts, vests. The children dressed in their Sunday best. The subway car was packed but not unpleasantly so. A few younger people from the Village were in the car dressed more fashionably bohemian – no sense of a Saturday going out night, but the sensibility of a very special family occasion that meant something to each immigrant in that car. The foreigners brought sandwiches to eat on the train, or to save for the walk to the expressway bordering the East River. You could feel the excitement from the people in the car, something that was new and precious to their second chosen country. One could simply imagine a refugee from the Middle East running across borders to find a safe haven where he would not be shot outright at the border. The majority of the people in the subway car were immigrants from Queens, people who had to live frugally because they earned only modest wages as in-home help, delivery boys, and day workers. Each family had a background quite different from my Midwestern background which was poor but protected, and left many very clannish – entire families living in one section of the State. New York City is where people came into America. If they did not pass through Ellis Island they had to pass through something very much like it. But since they were now American citizens or soon to be American citizens this Fourth of July meant a lot to them. They wore their Sunday best. The general feeling in the subway car was one of quiet awe, of family pride, of HOPE for a good future. Children were carrying small American flags in their hands ..... the smallest baby on the shoulders of a man was carrying the American flag. He had no idea what it was about, but his parent sure did and the quiet honor of a really very special new freedom where everything would improve for them if they worked hard enough was a real dream, and very likely attainable if they were willing to work hard, learn well, pay attention, if given the chance by the businesses that ran New York City, the politicians that ran New York City and the neighbors who would accept them into their apartment buildings. And in 1993 that was a given. That was a right. They were welcomed as part of a very necessary workforce that New York City depended on.

I was immediately buoyed up by the wave of mutual respect, friendliness, interaction and engagement between the classes of people on that train. That's how New York City was when I arrived.

We finally arrived at the most Eastern side of Manhattan and emerged from the last subway stop. We climbed to the street. There were hoards of people on the street, every nationality, all beautifully dressed roughly half of them carrying small American flags. We were all headed in one group toward the far East side of Manhattan to Roosevelt Drive which had been closed that night. Once past the city blocks and stores the crowd thinned out only a little. There was virtually no conversation except for asking directions and making sure we were all heading the right way. We arrived at the expressway onramp and the mass circled steadily up the onramp to Roosevelt Drive. We were met by thousands of people already there who had chosen their spots; we joined them and stood waiting for the fireworks to begin.

The crowd was orderly. The crowd was excited. The crowd was respectful. The national anthem played to open, and in the mass of immigrants it was very hard for me not to cry. To be a small part of such a lovely city; to be a small part of such a wonderful country. To have immigrants that within a few months had joined you in New York City and were sharing their dream of America with your dream of a New York City America - simply overwhelming and humbling. Elliot stood close. The tears were running from my eyes. The tears were running from Elliot's eyes. The patriotism for this incredible country was palpable. The new immigrants joy reminding me of how special the U.S.A. was, how special New York City was. Elliot remembered more tragedy. He remembered guarding the war criminals at Nurenbuerg; he remembered being a sharp shooter for the U.S. army protecting the telephone lines for the allies in WWII. Yes it is a great country, to be cherished and protected and fought for if necessary. And I, Edith Schult, was the newest immigrant to this wonderful city.

It was almost impossible not to be moved by the immigrants. They made me remember how great America is. How great New York City is. Contrast that to 2018, and my blood runs cold. We can never forget where we have been. It's the only map back to reality to the wonderfully free, balanced, prosperous America inhabited by America's John Q. Public. That means all of us.

Spreading Manure

October, the air is crisp and clear, the colors are rich in the trees, brown on the sleeping earth getting ready for the blanket of snow that will rest on everything later.

You spend your day out in this lovely field, no one is with you . . . who likes to fertilize the earth with the excrement of cattle? – but it is a job to be done and one that has its own beauty in the doing

Each forkful has its own weight and aroma as you place it in the spreader . . . it's not a bad aroma, but musky, braced with the nip in the fall air, very pure in its strength

You pull the tractor and spreader out from the barnfill and head toward the edge of the field, where you will start first

The fences go by, a bird flies up in front of you from the quiet racket you create as your vehicle crunches over the field. There's just a little frost out there, you can see your breath as you breeze along in the silence of the morning at 5 a.m.

It's crisp and exhilarating, better than a jog through the parks of a major city, your own quiet world to dream in, to meditate in, very close to God and what really matters in this intrinsic part of civilization . . .

Each round you go, each wagonful you load keeps you very close to God's earth, very close to God. This quiet, this calm cannot be experienced by the misfortunate who live in the metropolis, those who would be embarrassed by the elementalness of cattle excrement.

Spreading Manure

Oscar

My little friend, you who so faithfully wait on me each eve,
entertain me with your good humor delight me
with your presence as I watch you in your search for
that speck of dust, or that cockroach completely
bemused and entertained in your concentration . . .

The simplicity of your spirit, its truthfulness and
sweetness and honesty completely unruffled
by all that goes around you completely unaware
in your concentration of the melancholy you lift from my shoulders . . .

What has your day been in my absence?—a conversation
with the neighbor, gazing balefully at the big black dog that
barks so incessantly and dumbly through our kitchen window,
smelling the crisp air outside in the shade of the grape leaf
your eyes focused in the deep concentration of the outside world . . .

Or resting supine on my bed contemplating the ceiling,
as you loll about basking in the warmth and glow of our company,
safe from intruders and the cacophonous brayings of the day in your concentration of this moment . . .

Meditation

You sit there so proud and mute on my pillow like a small Buddha plump on his throne, pondering the timeless quiet of this hour; delicate pinkness, comforting sweetness without malice of the waking populace.

Quiet and serene watching humanity about is business like so many mice scattering before the noise of intimidation.

Total Equipoise, nothing ruffling that luxurious exterior for whatever insignificant man-made interruption.

Sensual warmth exuding to me in my observation

Of this langorous contemplation of humanity; warm and snug against the ravages of the world outside.

Storm

The bowels of heaven issue forth their black bolts of rage, impinging on the shell of the earth, massive,

Such power covers man, each infinitesimal second of life –

Never venting itself, save for

Raining on the parched waiting earth,

Sweeping the chaff and waters in its way, brushing us with it into its heart–

This connection, regenerating our senses like a depleted cell . . . the power, the might of this energy.

Be swept away into its eye and lifted to the heights of our humaness at the whim of this glorious charger –

This steed of the nighttime, the cool wind on your face

As you plunge into blackness.

Rain

Gently rain falls at my window, drawing me forth into a warm cordial completely new day,

Walking out into a new world, fresh our most primitive being touches with the earth,

We are consumed by this sumptuous warmth enveloping us, comforting us, blotting out old fatigues, old sorrows, heavy sadness that somehow would jar our waking self in the glare of the sunlight,

Out into the darkness, the welcoming darkness of the rain, the gift of the gods, - how long has this earth revolved with the watchful guiding eye of the gods,

Our connection with the universe is separate in the sunlight, distant; we are at one with this universe, this entity, this unknown.

The gentle, soft rain of this day pulls us into the night of our essence, where secrets lurk, where the wonderment of our humanity rests serene,

This gentle serene rain connecting the pit of our being with the core and power of the universe, our small dot of existence a mere spec of protoplasm in eternalness . . . .

Going Home

The phone rings. A worried voice tells you, "He's in the hospital for observation." Symptoms recounted. Heart attack. No – can' t be. He's indestructible. The center of your universe can't fade from you. Much too sturdy, hearty, healthy. Has to be influenza or something like it. You reassure that worried voice and vow to call the hospital after the test results are back. No use now, can't tell anything. You hang up, go about your business. Must walk – anything to dispel the fear and worry – and kill time.

Ironic–kill time–45 minutes later a different, resigned voice calls you. Too late. All the years you feared you wouldn't be there for his passing flood over you. Too much to absorb, you fall back silent in tears. All those years of worry culminated in that phone call. Hardly worthy or representative of your universe dissolving away. Somehow a friend organizes you enough to get on a plane, call your employer, pack your clothes. You don't see or feel anything. You are in transit, as you were not between those two fateful phone calls. Connections are bad; 2.5 hour layover in a distant city 'til you are home. Another friend waits the 2.5 hour layover with you "How's everything?" You talk about the mundane activities in both your lives, your new love life. Terrible to think of those things now. Life simply cannot change that fast. It as. How do you comfort each other? Communication misses. You don't connect. Time to leave. With so little having been felt you leave your friend. Thirty minutes 'til you face his widow and your sister. What will you say? What can you say? Practical matters keep you going. Did you pack everything? Will the luggage get lost? At the airport two sad faces search you out for some sign of hysteria. You embrace and the tears don't come. Absolutely mute. Twenty minutes by car. As you drive, they repeat the story for the 20th time that day. You acknowledge it, but don't absorb.

Home, the door opens, the house is empty. He'll come to the door with the paper in his hand to help you with your bags like always. No. Nothing. Maybe he's sleeping on the sofa. Still nothing. You unpack, feed your tired, frightened cat and sit up until 4 a.m. talking with his widow, and your sister until you are tired enough to sleep.

Three hours later you wake. Many decisions today. Casket to pick out, flowers to decide, pall bearers to call. And – the ultimate meeting with your father before they take away his uniqueness. You must see him alone, just as you used to – to say good-bye.

You see him laid out on a slab with no color, cold and still. You touch his hand. It's real, not just an terrible abstract rumor. Little remains of that beautiful spirit behind those sleeping eyes; but still there is a shadow, a trace, and oh so many memories. You finally feel. How could you have waited?

Your last conversation with him was a week before. Optimistic, concerned, "How's Skipper doing?" "As well as can be expected. He's getting old you know." "Yes, if he makes it through spring he'll have a nice summer. We'll keep our fingers crossed." "Ja, well this is getting expensive for you. Take care of yourself." "Ja, Daddy, take care, I love you." "Ja".

Hundreds of people come to mourn. What can you say? Everything is one hollow blur. The story is repeated a hundred times as if with each retelling you will be able to feel the pain so much that it will somehow set everything right. After the last person, you leave, say goodnight to your Father and go home to feed Skipper. You see Skipper and tell him the story; he knows as only an animal can know. You hold him and weep. His dog. His barn. His land. This was his domain. A domain that you could not embrace for your life's work. These are your roots, but to grow, you had to break from them, and yet something got lost in the growing. This is the pain you must face. This is the dying. You tuck the dog in for the night, close the barn door and go to the house and to bed – not to sleep, but to think.

The funeral takes place for the mourners. It is hollow, - the reality is in my Father's barn. We all try very hard to comfort each other in our shared unreality. The last shovel of earth is thrown on the grave. The evening fog rolls in, and we stand alone – feeling. Everything was done properly. He would have been pleased. Now the practicality of living day to day hits us squarely. As inexorable as death is, so is life. Two faces of the same coin.

The Lone Line Tree

The last vestige remaining of the original farm that is now in shambles, requiring yellow metal posting notices on surrounding fence posts to indemnify the children of the original owner from any lawsuit that might arise from any predatory hunter who invades the private posted land that remains of the original homestead.

The children of the original farmer who are still alive – though living in a distant Midwestern town, hoping that the fences hold another season so they don't have to fight winter roads to inspect and possibly deflect any court summons that would interrupt their current schedule.

The inability to simply sell out-right the remaining homestead thereby cutting childhood memories and ties to the land you grew up on, you worked on, mourned on when members of your family died one by one.

The life force that keeps going as you age knowing that you will have to provide for your children, after you are dead, divide properties fairly, prepay funerals and hire the attorney who will help finalize any memories of the homestead that no longer exists.

The life force that in spite of man's neglect, keeps growing, absorbs nutrition from the hard rocky ground that is left. Shades of the Joad family on its trip westward to California. Wisconsin in Spring and Summer is equally vibrant, but the winters last six months.

One day the field will be smoothed over into one property with the lot next to it. Some wealthy corporate farmer will buy the remaining heirs out at a high enough price for them to leave the memories behind in the cold.

One day that lone line tree will be pulled up by its roots with heavy farm equipment and steel chains, which will obliterate the entire line that divided the adjoining properties.

Until then, Lone Line Tree, you will remain the highest visible point for all to see from any distance less than three miles, unless a snowmobile destroys your roots first.

You will rule the vista for all people to see when they pass if they are not speeding past too quickly in their cars and trucks to notice.

Sunday

From the days of our youth we work to celebrate Sunday,

Sunday, the luxurious sunny, slow langorous time,

Years of fresh green grass, sparkling streams, jumping fish, serenity, Sunday, the family day, children tumbling in the hay, kittens hiding in sleep, warm, snug, safe, quiet,

Sunday, at twilight, the scent of clover moist on our face, the world calm, waiting for the week's rude awakening

Sunday, the later years, aged like ripe chees, richly pungent, full, An era planned for and earned with an entire lifetime's labor, -- Not to be spent alone, pondering past sorrows, but to be shared,

By two who have known a lifetime and understood its ransom, To be shared, the serenity, the beauty, the calm russetness of the remaining Sundays of time.

Christmas

Christmas comes but once a year; with it joy and lots of cheer. That's what the authorities say. Why of all the days in the year has this one been singled out?

The family unit in America has changed drastically in the last 100 years. We no longer depend on horse and sleigh to get about. We no longer live, several family units to a house with extended family relatives. Son and daughter go off to college and the family unit breaks up, leaving an empty nest. Schools and careers pull people to all points on the globe. Somehow our lives get lived at an incredible pace – too fast – too superficial – too goal centered. And yet somehow at the core of each of us is the memory of one wonderful Christmas when we were young and protected and unknowing enough to be really happy. Ignorance is bliss all right. Usually that memory goes back many years when we didn't have so much, things were tight financially, simpler, and yet as children we had no knowledge of this. It was just the simple pleasure of here and now. No painful unhappiness to surface inconveniently, with only the need to be exorcised like some shadowy demon.

Yet, each year we put ourselves through this ritual like the lemmings march to the sea. Somehow we hope that the feelings we hold back, the communication that is never spoken, the love that is undemonstrated, the closeness that is not felt for the other 364 days will somehow be set right on this one day. Instead, as we sit around the tree, we remember those of use who are dead that we didn't say those things to, we think of the killer plane ride home, the gifts that aren't as special as we want to give, and all the other Christmases that weren't so happy – and we notice the gilt chipping off the plastic star and think how many more Christmases will we share with our

loved ones before they are gone. And will we ever recapture that closeness that was once there? Christmas is only 1 in 365 days that we communally try to touch and reach each other. Why can't we wish that for the other 364, and consciously act on that intention?

Christmas serves to point up exactly how alone we are – apart from each other. That loneliness is more acute for the immediate companionship of family and friends. Whether we like it or not, each year beyond the cradle we lose more innocence, struggle for our purposes in life harder, acquire more hurts and gather more distance between us and those we love. That is the price for becoming our own unique individual. Every bruise and sensitivity we earn ourselves. It must be so.

Perhaps it must always be so. A richer fuller life is better than a vacuous, regulated and unemotional life. We must weep to know joy, we must hate to know love, we must lay bare our side to have strength. If we did not have the wealth of emotional resources to draw on, we would be only half alive. If Christmas is upsetting, face it, vent the feeling, respond. Express those submerged hurts, and reach out beyond them, beyond this one day.

A Portrait of My Grandmother

Going home on the holidays generally means a visit with your grandparents. When you were a child, things were more balanced and comfortable for this occurrence. Now, however, the locale has changed. That once lucid grandparent is now in a nursing home with two lame hips that no longer support the weight and age that time has placed on them.

Nursing homes always have that not so fresh, but yet sanitary odor about them. The heat is quite suffocating. These sensations assault you like a blast furnace as you walk in the door.

You bring your gifts. You help her open them. Her eyes gaze at them in wonderment, like a small child on his first Christmas. But yet, no recognition of your face or your particular place in her family. She still is the head of that family, if only in exile, - the heart of that family does exist, - even though her children are pained at her senility, and reminded that some day too, they will finish out their days thus. That is not the only pain. The person to lean on and turn to when they were afraid of the dark, or of things, people , and most dramatically – relationships. So we sing the carols with her, weeping as we do for the tenderness that is there, the tenderness that is part of this grand matriarch, - even though she is totally unaware of the effect of her childlike sweetness.

These are also the times that the culprit who had to put her in the home feels the most guilt. The word culprit is certainly not my choice of description. However, it most accurately describes the guilt that this individual feels in the pit of her stomach. It also describes the passive guild that is felt by the rest of the immediate family at having left this very distasteful task to that one lone individual. We are human. It is very human . . . to want to feel that, in your own eyes, you are not a bad person. . . especially when the "problem" is your own mother. The trauma that goes into the decision to place your parent in a nursing home is one of the heaviest that any of us has to bear. There is so much love and the need, - and want to have that person with us in our own home, - in our personal care. That in the pit of your stomach you know (albeit not so correctly) that no one will care for your mother with as much love, skill, or devotion as you. And that for you to turn her away to a stranger is the final damning rejection and hatefulness that she is twice your weight (dead weight), cannot walk or remember even at times when to eat. Something in you says, "She gave me life. I must do the same for her and sustain her life and happiness as long as I am able. Any other treatment of her (in my eyes) is totally selfish and reprehensible."

The only cure for all this ill-will I know of is time. That is what has made this particular holiday so bittersweet. Time has passed, Others close to us are not with us. Somehow the precious few minutes with this wizened old woman brings everything back to normalcy, - to a time in our childhood and our innocense. It is a time when that individual, the culprit, in her heart knows that everythin is as right as it ever will be again in her life. She knows that everything is in place, and at peace. She is richer for having been through the fire, much richer than the less involved, less experienced of her family.

Maestro – A Dedication

That special smile, even when I fall short,
That subtle belief that supports me even when I doubt,
The total acceptance even when I bare my weakness,

The comfortable giggle at a small shared fraction of communication,
The broad laughter at a totally lascivious joke,
The happiness at an attempt well taken,

The honor of the most beautiful art,
The respect in realizing that art,
The pursuit of that perfection in
The company of a kindred spirit,

The realization that there is someone
Out there like me,
With serious intent and dedication
To an art much greater than the
Mentality of the masses,
Who wants to see it flourish
And transform humanity.
For all you gifts,
I thank you my Friend

Grape Leaf

Crisp Sunday morning, light passing through transparent life, gold tinged, radiant, snapping brilliantly to Autumn's rhythm.

How lovely, the fraction of time, to spend in this clarity, this peacefulness while others in church listen to the moth-eaten fusty harangues of the elders, the churchmen – of what God is.

God is in that lovely gold grape leaf that moves so slightly in the cool morning air.

He is the silent cool clarity of this moment.

Looking skyward, the clouds so gentle, mighty yet varporizing with approach.

He is not some icon that we can touch and refinish: distort with our dogmas – no matter who preaches.

He is all around us if we care to look, if we let our senses sniff Him from the air, touch Him in the earth and see Him in that leaf.

Aw-struck, I turn from my window, from that grape leaf so exquisite, to my dull interior. He is there too, only I seek Him there with Jaundiced eyes, with pain, loneliness, and past hurts.

Somehow that sense of the grape leaf I must hold true to myself. It is not solid, dense and futile as cement, but at its base is enough life's essence to lie dormant and later come to fruition another day.

That Juice of life – our essence to fuel the daily struggle of our existence. Just like the leaf our daily struggle may pallor, but given one's faith in the golden Juice, our dormancy will pass.

Dormancy serves its purposes for reflection;

26

Without reflection and self-search no fruits will be born.

Everything was put on this earth for a purpose. Living things bear fruit. After dormancy, the fruit is richer and fuller for having rested. We must take our token form that leaf.

Gray(Grey??)

People softly come and go Talking of Michelangelo. Day in, day out, every day

Of every year, every minute of every hour, every second of every minute. Where is the future; I'm too tired to battle it; it seems so futile to struggle on to who knows what?

So tired you muddle down into the quicksand to be swallowed up and drowned in the mire.

Where's the Quixotic optimism that somehow surfaces enough to go on? It took the day off. Maybe I should take the rest of my life off. To sleep or to dream, dream for what?

Impatience with the development of destiny makes me very tired indeed, tired to death.

Boredom, - that's death. I'm not alone in this assessment. To kill time, it is a sin, yes a sin, but kill it we all do in dead-end jobs, dead-end relationships that drain you inch by inch of any vibrancy that was there. Will it come back, or do I allow myself to sink into grayness?

Black and white aren't bad; they're definite at least. But that awful grey gray, blandness that suffocates any creativity or desire.

They say that when one ceases to desire one has reached the ultimate enlightenment. Either that or they are simply pickled with the numbness that creeps in with making ends meet, making do, compromising to people who outrank you, out-earn you, not necessarily outsmart you, but they hold the full house in their hands and you hold the sand as it slips through your fingers.

The futility of it all. To spend a lifetime like this without hope of anything better; suicide would be a better, at least it would be a positive act.

But I don't have the energy or courage for that. Maybe Skinner is right, maybe we should have that final option when we are no longer of use to the earth, or the rest of humanity, or to ourselves.

Who can tell when that usefulness is finally ended, exactly when - without bias?

Equinox

Walking out into the clouded grey ominous air the crunch of icicle leaves beneath my feet,

Looking into that sky that surrounds me watching so balefully,

Adding weight to my already heavy shoulders, looking over the choppy rough waters, seeing no clarity, only blackness,

To drown in that blackness and obliterate myself so I can vaporize into the clouds above, feel their coldness, their dampness.

No warmth, no place warm to sit before a friendly fireplace, shuddering and shivering beneath my coat I look around,

All are mated, paired . . . . I wonder if they have that warmth I seek or do they feel the coldness of that wide atmosphere glaring at me?

Walk through the once green grass, now hardened earth for comfort, yes, even in this cold earth with the snows nearing there is comfort, if not warmth,

So the earth must now fall asleep and slumber beneath its white blanket. Such deadness, everything held in suspension for how long, - a few months perhaps. How long will my heart be held in similar suspension, comfortable alone, but cold, very cold and soggy.

An endless lifetime of this dullness, my life only to be an eternal span of winters, void of joy, full of drudgery and ceaseless work.

Vacumm

People drifting to work; a job leading Nowhere. A year of weeks, Years of Nothingness.

Feeding our faces with the frustration of time ill-spent.

Enclosed in our shells, waiting for opportunity to peck through and break the isolation of our Futility.

Why?

The Masses who sell out for the Buck to afford the few minutes away from the Grind.

The Ratio of time spent grinding to the Time, reaping its meager Rewards.

Surely, Life is more than this. We insulate ourselves from Living, -- from Tasting completely

Insulation – Isolation

Black Dog

You came as a puppy, full of joy and tumbling all over the children, happy in their company.

Do you remember those times shared, or do you forget, as I see you sitting dully in the corner of your cement yard?

How long has it been that you've seen your children or the mistress that thought you so cuddly? You pass each day, -day by day, looking out at the rest of the world as it walks past your gate, growling in frustration at it.

Do you feel sorrow, black dog, for what is no longer, do you remember, or does each day pass as something wholly new and interesting?

The voices over the fence, just out of reach to you, but not out of hearing, do you ever dream of green fields, or is that beyond your comprehension?

Daily, your children come in to feed and water you but, no tumbling or play, you are now big and overgrown and your playful overtures not so welcome to their small size. So –

They leave you to meet their friends, to play with each other just beyond your reach, your need.

Black Dog, winter will be here soon, Will you come inside out of the cold, or will you shiver outside on cement?

Will you come into Christmas and join the laughter that you so faintly remember when you were young, or will you look in on your family through the window as the cold bites at your feet?

The Handsome Man in Modest Work Clothes

I greet you on the bridge every morning, laden down with hundreds of plastic bottles, empty, used up, less than clean, the refuse of society, the bottom rung of existence, society's throw-aways, but your daily subsidy, rain, snow or sleet, bare hands clutching the huge bag,

Your handsome face peering out from beneath an old baseball cap, a smile of greeting and a nod. How you keep going mystifies me,

Your courage when you entered the country illegally across a hot endless border, ducking fat cat authorities totally unacquainted with the work you slaved at; taking bribes to look the other way, bribes that took you years to acquire,

The cold drizzling rain, bleak day on the bridge, the bag of plastic grip slipping, unending fatigue mounting the countless miles you treck into Queens, the safe, mostly white yet purile fearful populace; they will give you the few sheckles for your effort

You secrete your meager belongings in the bridge framework, out of sight to most; the bridge your home, a refrigerator box your bedroom until mold forces you to lay on the pavement next to skeleton buildings covering with whatever handy, newspapers, old blankets while the powerful step over you or alternatively deny your very existence, the murky sky overhead ...

A good weekend, a kind referral to others who have preceded you to the big city who live in illegal basements a damp roof overhead with ten people who share a once a week bath and impromptu family for a day yielding a sense of belonging if only for a few hours, emotional renewal for awhile, the next morning's dreadful renewed life struggle with the city for the job, any job as elusive as your language barrier

Waking Dawn

Waking to the birds singing chatter; blue light filtering through the blinds. Gentle cool morning air; refreshing to the skin;

Calm, clear quiet time; soft breeze embracing my skin; total stillness in my mind, but yet a Beethoven Sonata surfacing from my memory – a dream perhaps – a lovely soulful second movement.

Free floating remembrance of an intrusive phone call from a friend of a past life wishing to connect, fearful of being alone – running hard. Facing the day of reality ahead with the mundane day-to-day happenings of big business, of the business of life, the business of survival – the very grist of life that propels us forward, the very stimulus that makes us dream, strive, create and live *now.*

Cool lovely morning to reflect, ramble through our thoughts, process our lives, integrate our sensibilities before the noise of the day creeps in, before the demands are made, before the very things we try to block out and rise above bring us crashing to earth to ground us in the human struggle.

The few clear moments before the roar of the vast waking city silences the pristine song of the lovely birds... the metallic groan of the grinding threshing machine that we must face head on.

Wisconsin Flashback

Schmetterling, Papillon,
Butterfly, flutterby, Monarch,
the king of the Decorative bugs,
Lighting on the wild flowers,
Matching the orange Tiger Lilies
That grow as weeds along the
Roadway in Wisconsin,

All the lovely foliage laden with,
Enhanced by, nurtured by and
And fertilized by the ubiquitous
Butterfly, so delicate and lovely
And fragile, only to be seen precisely
By some bug collector who will
Destroy its life to look closer.
I have yet to see a Monarch in New York City,
but then New York
City so concrete bound,
Is hardly the gentlest of places
For such fragile beauty to flourish.

An Observation

On a Sunday afternoon, after a morning's three hour rehearsal in town, I decided to drive back into Manhattan to determine how long it would take to bike to work, to bike to ballet and then return to Queens. I found ballet to be 45 minutes away on bicycle and slightly longer by train. New York services have been hit by the economy and so on any given day you can be left high and dry by the subways, and I had a nearly disastrous commute to a dental appointment the week before. Knowing New York's Mass Transit Authority at this stage - I expected them to start jerking us around so I prepared in advance for the likelihood.

On my way back over the 59th Street Bridge to Queens, a Eurasian man (he could not have been more than 150 pounds) drove by on a motorized scooter no bigger than a child's push scooter – only there was a small motor on the back and the man had slightly more than a foot span in length and less that a foot span in width to stand on (in other words roughly the space you would have on a skateboard – only the scooter was motorized). On his head he wore a sturdy looking red metal helmet, and strapped to his back was a red backpack designed to carry a dog, and as he passed me I noticed that the lid was open on the backpack and a small 10 pound brown dachshund mix was looking back at me – his ears flying in the wind. Since two years earlier I had crashed a small razor scooter (unmotorized) into the base of the bridge on the hair pin turn at the bottom, I shuddered at the possibility of the dog being thrown out of the backpack as the owner blithely motored on over the bridge.

The two of them left me in the dust since I only had my own leg power to climb the steep incline on my mountain bike. At the crest of the bridge, the man had stopped and pulled to the side. His head was pushed between the joining protective fence sections as he looked up the East River at the view. His hands were solidly on the scooter handles, one foot was on the scooter – the other on the bridge. And the dog? The dog was in the process of curling up to sleep in the backpack. As I drove by I realized the backpack was rigged with a nylon harness, water and snack trays. Only in New York would you likely see that. In other cities, there would be a young child in the backpack. But in New York, people live alone with their pets.

Why do people move to New York? A very good question. Some leave their birth homes – whether in the U.S. or Europe or Asia or Russia because New York represents the gateway to America. So many times on my various returns from Europe on a plane loaded with passengers, when we collectively saw the Statue of Liberty and the ribbon of diamonds that delineate the street of Broadway that runs the length of Manhattan, there was a spontaneous round of applause and cheering. New York is indeed a jewel of a city. It has the very worst in it and the very best in it.

It forces you to broaden your response to different nationalities and races, to different beliefs and ideas, to different ways of doing things, different ways of being. New York is also where so many European traditions have their American residence. World-class, world-famous musicians live and perform there. The finest artists study there, the finest dancers. New York City boasts two music conservatories with world class reputations. The theater is there – and live, the Metropolitan Opera, New York City Opera, ABT and New York City Ballet. It is also the place you can be exposed to the finest teachers of every stripe, and the price generally is affordable and it's only a subway ride away. I have a Bachelors and Masters Degree in Music, but my real musical development has occurred in New York – and I continue to grow.

It is however wall-to-wall cement. And I grew up on a farm in Wisconsin and worked out in the fields consistently with my family –

it was a beautiful way to grow up. My original home in Wisconsin will always be my grounding point. I live very simply in New York and like most musicians and artists I work a straight job to support my artistic pursuits and do run-outs to perform. Above all, New York City is a way to grow artistically. I have learned so much about life and people as a result of living in New York.

I come to Wisconsin to relax and recharge my batteries, but New York is where my life force is inspired to struggle to grow from week to week, year to year.

The January 23, 2016 Blizzard / The Ambulance

I had hustled to get my house set up for the presumed upcoming blizzard on the Thursday and Friday before the storm came in late Friday night.

So, I was set. On Saturday I just had to run to the post office early to pick up a package and get home fast. At 9:30 am when I got home from my post office trip, I noted that visibility was less than half a block, and the wind was picking up.

I drank some hot chocolate and settled in with a day of Law and Order reruns and calling my family and friends at a distance. Normally I do that Sunday, but I had a rehearsal in town Sunday and it was anyone's guess how mobile I would be after the snow hit, so I started calling family and friends Saturday to keep Sunday open.

I looked out my kitchen window and noticed an ambulance mired in the snow. Two guys were trying to unearth the vehicle, and there were two Eastern Indians trying to dig out in front of the ambulance to get it going.

I made another phone call, and figured if four men couldn't figure a way out, well then, when I went to the train station to see if there would be any service the next morning, I would see if I could help. I made one more phone call, then I bundled up and went outside. I walked over to the ambulance and asked one of the men digging if they knew how to "rock a car". One thought he might know how.

I asked them if they wanted some help, explaining that I had grown up on a farm in Wisconsin and had dug my way out far worse messes than their ambulance was in. The two Eastern Indians had stopped digging and decided to watch. I walked to the back of the vehicle and noticed there was another Eastern Indian on a guerney inside the ambulance, and calculated that they had run the medical equipment for a solid hour + gas for that hour, and had gotten the ambulance tires really hot from all the tire spinning, so they could run out of gas unless someone helped them out of their mess.

So I noticed that they had dug out in back of the ambulance and in front of the ambulance, and there was a lump of iced over packed up snow just in back of the right front wheel. I asked "Which way do you want to go, forward or backward?" They replied "forward". And I said, "You will never make the grade from a dead start with a vehicle whose center of weight is so high. 1st gear is the most powerful gear, but REVERSE beats all the gears for slow power."

So they readjusted mentally, and I noticed that they were willing to listen to me. I said, "everybody except the driver up front to the nose of the vehicle." The two Eastern Indians who had been digging kept watching. I explained to the more eager of the two paramedics (yellow jacket), that the driver had to precisely apply the speed and keep it very steady and stable in reverse, and the three of us would push like crazy upon the driver actually engaging the accelerator. I told yellow jacket that Crescent was a one-way street going south, and he replied "We can go the wrong way with an ambulance if we run our flashing lights." So I had a good idea how it would work the best.

We backed the ambulance over the frozen lump of snow and kept going in reverse........ and yelled at the driver to keep going and not stop until we were in the middle of Crescent Street where it had been plowed clear – there was no traffic – so we were good to go. Then I yelled to stop immediately half way through the move since the driver was right on edge of going off the roadbed and off the asphalt. If we got stuck there we would need a tow truck to get us out!

I ran to the back of the ambulance and jumped across a 3 foot snowbank to the other side of the vehicle to see where the right rear wheel was. We were safe. I talked to yellow jacket and explained that the driver should carefully feed in first gear but NOT turn the front wheels until we were going, and once we got going he could gradually turn left onto Crescent. The three of us pushed hard after yellow jacket yelled at the driver to "go".

We stopped in the middle of a clear road 2 blocks from the hospital and it was all down hill to get there. Everyone except the patient and the two Eastern Indians who were leaning on their snow shovel handles watching us jumped out of the ambulance and hugged me. I explained that I had had a cardiac arrest in June, but I had a defibrillator embedded in my chest in case my heart stopped. There was no damage to my heart. Yellow jacket freaked out. "Can we drive you someplace", and I said "no – I have to see if I will have to walk into Manhattan tomorrow morning so I have to get to the train station." The other paramedic stood before me and said, "You have performed an incredible mitzvah tonight. How can we ever thank you enough." "Maybe it's time for me to reciprocate for the wonderful medical attention I got to save my life. We're even. Have a good life."

They drove off, and I walked between the two Eastern Indians who had begun to shovel again and wished them a good night on my way to the train station.

I probably should have gone out earlier to bail them out, but I figured they would assume if I had gone earlier that this was an easy fix, and anyone could have done it. I chocked this up to women power and having had a wonderful father who never ever limited me as I grew up.

SJHassel

Alison –

This modest care package is something I hope you will take with you to college.

The purse (decorative monk's bag actually): Is merely something colorful, artistic and funky that you can use or give to a friend or use as a prop. I'm using it rather than wrapping the care package.

The framed picture: A quick water color drawing of a French painter complete with beret. This is your reminder to never forget why you are sacrificing so much to get your MFA. You will now be in a different milieu where there are inherent struggles, some pitfalls surely and hopefully much inspiration in a setting where you will be with like-minded young people. The drawing is clearly an *artiste* which is someone you will become, which is what you feel you are from the core on out, which is the identity you must have so that you do not suffocate in your skin. Hopefully the little drawing will be a kind of touch stone when things are not going so well, when doubts begin to clutter your head, when and if politics raises its nasty head that could slow down or stop your artistic growth and forward momentum. The little painting will remind you that there can be ***no doubts***. There will just be the grounded surety that you are an actor and that you are *where you belong*.

The silk shawl: A second-hand gift from a stunning Armenian man who *came* before Elliot swept me off my feet. I have kept this shawl in the back of my closet. It immediately jerks me back to my first year in New York City, and it represents to me all of the forward-looking artistic potential that I was able to enjoy and grow into. It represents the beginning of my artistic journey in NYC – a journey which has not stopped but continues in ever new mystifying ways. I am always reminded to look forward to future artistic development and as long as I have energy, I know I will become a great artist in whatever path that presents itself that I follow.

I now pass this talisman on to you to keep in your closet, to visit every now and again to remind yourself of when your *real journey* began, how far you have to go, and how wide your potential can expand as a result of the risk you are taking.

Finally, you have my best wishes for your success. You must *ALWAYS FOLLOW YOUR DREAM*. You have only one life. Live it so you have no regrets – and *ALWAYS PUSH THE ENVELOPE!*

You go girl! Best wishes – Sue

POETRY WRITTEN WHILE LISTENING TO CLASSICAL MUSIC

(Medtner, Mozart, Debussy, Schumann, Satie)

Parnasus

Azure Blue waters lap at your shores
Blue water so transparent, you can see
The light sea shells on the ocean's floor,
The varied-color fishes swimming serenely beneath.

As we near the Island of your source,
The green shoreline emerging from the morning mist
Your white-gray top appearing first,
Then the grand rolling mass emerging as we dock.

Mountaintop of Greece where
Imagination was Born
Thoughts, words,
Spirit, Core, Color, Form and Sound

Aspiration of novices, who ascend
The very programmed, stepwise crabbing
Development to perfection
As Clementi observes from on high bemused.

Baby's First Steps

Grey mass, moving slowly
Steady through the grass
Momma in front - Baby at the heels
Snout clutching mom's tail
Slowly, steadily on wobbly legs
Moving with the troupe through the
Wide African plains

Grouped together, babies protected
By moms, halting, watchful
Lions giving wide berth to
The herd of modern gray mastodons
The ground vibrating with the weight of
Each muffled, steady, compressed step

Extended infancy of a 200 lb. child

Automaton

Magic leather box,
Tooled gold design, lavender warmth
Closed a curiosity – with Golden latch
Open the lid

A shimmering mirror pops up
And before the lid, a delicate porcelain
Figurine – Wind the key, the figure turns

Mauve tutu reflecting in the mirror,
Gold locks tumbling over white shoulders
Extended en point – two figures to watch
One real, the other illusion

Sparkling, glinting shimmer
Aurora borealis – delicate lights
Refracting glint as the figure pirouettes
In timeless, endless perfection
Ending only when we close the lid...

Snowfall

Grey day, over all lit, luminous

Over-white.....

Dull, yet brilliant white.... Damp air, heavy air

Shivering wet cold, but not ice - not frigid

Looking out from the window

Onto the grayness

First one flake, then another

Big flakes, unique flakes, heavy flakes

First a light cover

Flake, by flake by flake by flake....

Hexagonal, pentagonal, florid, intricate,

Each one of a kind

Slowly building a fluffy mass over the ground

A soft dense blanket of white....

Total quiet, mesmerizing.......

Nose pushed to the window

Taking in the whiteness as the

World outside turns to shimmering silver

Night Song

High above the snow line now melted
From the summer's warmth
Sheep and goats gamboling with kids at the side
Grazing on fresh green grass

The sun now setting – twilight approaching
The solitary youth sitting on the stoop of his hut
Gazing at the red gold streaking light as it fades
Watching as the village in the valley below
Fades into the dark
Taking in the cool night air as the dew begins to settle

The solitary pan-pipe, hand-made by firelight
It's mournful tune wailing in the clear night air
A haunting singular sound that wafts over the valley
Echoing in the mountains
Setting off the stars as they appear in the blackness of approaching night

Walk Around

New age, inventive age, brash age
Hobble skirts that constrict movement
Dance lifted from minstrel shows,
Walkers with water buckets for crowns

Parody of the Big House balls
Vertical pairing of two people with nimble
Golliwogg feet
Deft, sharp movements, vitality as they circle the floor
Audience agog

Transformed by Irene and Vernon
Chic reference of the time
Trend setters turning away from the romantic
Tristan Legend
Opulence, cloche hats, long beads, bobbed hair
Tail coats, dandified jabots and spats
New dance, new age, new DAY

Note: Reference to Irene and Vernon Castle – two dancers who invented the Castle Walk in the early 20th century.

Wunderkind

Prodigy at 6, discovered at 7

Breadwinner at 8

Sheer brilliant invention

Improvisational novice that thrilled the kings of Europe

Brash adolescent in silk trousers and white wig

Possessed of music so clear, concise, eloquent and elegant

Pure and deft in structure, with rollicking laughter embedded in its base

Observer, capturing humankind in every sung character

Sublime purity, simplicity and profundity

Immortality is the imprint we leave on the world

After we have passed

Your star twinkled quietly all too briefly as you lived

But the light from that one twinkling star illuminated

Music and humanity for all time

Departure

Sunday arrival at port
Destination of a long horse carriage journey
Leaving the familiar behind
Enormous ships, sails rolled
Coarse trunks jammed to overflowing
Perched on father's shoulder - a safe crow's nest

On the dock the vendors selling their wares
Fresh fruit, sausages steaming over the fire
The smell of fresh warm yeasty bread and fish

Looking out over the water that extends into the horizon
Glassy water, murky close, but blue and icy in the distance
Floods of people in strange dress, all different
Dark eyes, blue eyes, blond hair, black hair – every conceivable
Nation - the entire populace – waiting, ready, wondering

What is over the water? Who is over the water? Excited expectation
All from the comfort of a father's arms – mother at the side.

Telling Tales

Cousins sprawled on the beds
Children huddled on the floor
In a bedroom, far from the ears of adults
Darkness settling in – but not yet slumber time

Emma whispers a tale to Gretchen,
Gretchen cups her hand and retells the tale
To Billy. Billy giggles and retells the story quietly
To Hans. Hans repeats the tale to Joseph, and Joseph
Whispers the tale to Heidi

Heidi jumps up and shouts the story to everyone - the story is not the same
As when first told
Peals of laughter, children's mirth til tears run down cheeks.

A knock at the door – Auntie looks in sternly – more giggles
Time to sleep.....

Tag, You're It

Sunny Sunday in the orchard

Foliage, red apples

Baskets and ladders all about for harvest

Time to play

Children scattering like chicks over the rough ground

Pinafores with grass stains, rough and tumbling

Knickers and striped wool socks, running, gamboling

One child overtaking the other – a swift lunging tap

On the shoulder and a hasty retreat

Someone else has to chase

Girls hiding behind the trees and bushes catching their breath

Trying to be invisible

Here he comes - RUN

Cookie

Mother and grandmother over hot stove

Morning's work with batter – chocolate chips – nuts

Sweet warm, inviting odor

Interminable wait – 10 minutes – 5 minutes

Can I lick the spoon?

More cookies – dozens of cookies.

Tugging at mother's apron – a dark look in return

The breadboard laid out fully on the table

Cookies lined up 6 per row like tin soldiers – hot – too hot

Grossmutter with the long white flower print apron, full bodied

Engaging and welcoming like a warm bed

Can I have one?

Response: A broad grandmother's smile

And an unnoticed motherly assenting nod.

The New Puppy

Average day, nothing to expect

Father late from work

Where is he?

Mother holding supper, food turning cold

Long expectation, anticipation - mother alert

Daddy opens the door

Now we can eat.... Not yet

A game to play – something in the pocket – which one?

What is it?

Father places the small fur ball in the child's hands

It squeaks, tries to crawl.... Is it a frog?

No - The child's very own *first puppy*.

This day will never be forgotten – the happiest day in a child's life.

Sunday Service

Saturday night bath; early Sunday rise

Chores to do, chickens to feed

Fresh shirt, best knickers polished shoes.

Hair spit slicked down with precise center part

Uncomfortable collar; mother, sister, father

All gussied in their finest - total fussy discomfort

Sitting in a cold hard pew, loud organ, women's perfumes

Men at attention, children perfect – or they better be

Preacher mounts the pulpit, flowing robes sweeping behind him

Total GRAVITAS

Pompous, inflated, ***captive***.

Dreams

Child nestled in bed, soft white cheek on
Linen pillow, slumber, perfection
House quiet – mother looks in

Child moves, sighs
Dusk settles over the house, time for dreams
Quiet open meadow, cool flowing stream, a butterfly
Lights on the child's hand

Sun glows over the scene – the child and moth shimmering in the sun
Delicate, satiny, peaceful, quiet while the child softly slumbers
The sweet smell of tender youth wafts through the room

As the child's sleep conjures up the open meadow.

Camping

After a long day of camping, tramping through the fields
Fording the streams, child safely on father's shoulders
Mother with daughter in hand two paces behind

Dusk, time to eat, hot dogs to roast
Potato salad to ladle out, and marshmallows to roast for desert

Faces gold from the fire's light, laughing, talking, family
Together recounting the day, bone tired from the tramping
Totally content looking to a good night's sleep near the fire's warmth.

Don Quixote

Knight in shining armor

Doing good for all

Better than great, rescuer to the needy

Inspiration, aspiration

Pursuing a lofty mission rescuing the world

Tilting at windmills

Take care you don't fall off your horse!

Solemnity

Quiet perfect little girl thinking silently
Sitting by the window as the world ages each day
Thinking lofty thoughts

Quiet gazing soulful eyes deeper than the ocean darker than the night
Do you think of worlds beyond; lost in your thoughts solitary
Or are the day's events that ordinary

You do your homework, stack your books
Make your bed – all without prompting
Perhaps there are great profound things in your future
But for your age, first there is childhood

You are 8 going on 30

Lightning

Dark clouds build up, sky foreboding

Inside safe, family around

Cozy from the storm, kitten by the hearth

A bright flash – "Oh my. Are we safe?

Will it get me?" Run and hide, crawl beneath the bed under

Cover for safety – security

Quiet returns

Another flash – run for cover

Into mother's arms, safe, secure, protected – serene

Bedtime

Tucked in, mother retreats

Can I have a glass of water?

Mother comes, child chatters as mother strokes the

Busy brow crooning a lullaby softly

The child gazes up at his mother's face

The warmth of her hand calming, settling, soothing

A quiet sigh –

NOW mother can go to bed.

Wordsmith

Appropriate words, well-chosen words
Timely words; ideas not nailed down
Fleeting words

The best ideas spontaneous and pointed – concise not verbose

Will the ideas ever stop? Will the well run dry?

The poet's quest.

Country Fair

Small town, once-a-year happening, late summertime, the last hurrah before fall, Gather the jams, flowers, produce, that prize pie, the prize cow

The blue 4-H jacket, jump in the pickup

People from miles around crowd the small town

The closer you get, the harder to park any car,

Hot summer afternoon, blue skies, fluffy clouds; Calliope steaming its tunes through the air, Ferris wheel arching high overhead

The main gate, bright colors, over-alls, tank tops, shorts

Holiday, thousands of people, happy, vocal, seeing and being seen,

Friends and family reuniting for a week's event before the fall harvest,

Wonderful, bright peasant dirndls with embroidered white aprons, floral headdresses with bright streaming ribbons moving vigorously in the air as

The feet in bright ethnic shoes dance to the Slavonic rhythms

Men in their bright suspenders, jaunty hats a century old, white embroidered shirtwaists swing the gaily decked out women in arm to the gay tunes played on the fiddle, concertina, cornet, and whatever other instrument comes to hand, the rhythmic fall of 30 feet on the impromptu wood stage.

The audience gathering to take in the exuberance and joy of the troupe.

Bright happy cacophony!

Memories

Plaintiff English horn wailing out the memory of home, of long ago and far away, a lifetime ago. Memories, a tradition left in Europe in the countryside of the rolling orderly plains, beautiful green hills with orderly crops planted

Simple huts with thatched roofs, hand sewn clothes, sheds built for a few cattle, the nearest neighbor miles away, peaceful isolation outside the front gate - The biggest event, a carriage ride to the neighboring church on Sunday - Original purity of a nation before

The world destruction and uproot of a simpler life by the Great War

Before even the large towns were leveled and re-built. European homeland left for the new American Midwest, seeking a similar-looking land, a similar rural setting, a similar simplicity, but not quite finding it.

The new country, vigorous, positive, neighborly with strange new customs or lack of customs. Total reinvention of the family, of the farm, of the land use. Bright, brash, noisy busy overwhelming cities. Join the fray or go under, mix in and rise to the top of the new society while maintaining distant European roots that fade as each year passes, only to be re-lived and remembered from an old yellowed, dog-eared photograph of a clan that no longer exists, which has been transplanted by a new, busier more affluent life in America.... The plaintiff folk-tune a very distant memory surfacing periodically bringing a tear to the eye.

Memories

Marie and Zoltan

Fruition of first meeting as children. Initial shy, embarrassed attraction, children of long-time neighbors and friends, that first day that the electricity sparked between. Long-termed loyalty, solid mutual interests, familial history binding the pair over many years

An inevitable progression, with only the interruption of military service; Marie hoping for the safe return, building her chest of linens, stitch by stitch over the years

Zoltan, returning home, decked out, handsome, worldly, changed.

Marie, hoping the change not too great, hoping the change will not reject

Time with family to recover the essence before the changes, incorporating the changes, rounding out and maturing

Zoltan no longer needing to impress, Marie longing to be impressed again. Years to regroup to reconstitute. Years to re-evaluate, to blend a life that has moved on during an absence..... the unsureness of that time, the fear of love lost...... all a fleeting memory. As Zoltan and Marie emerge from church, her white veil blowing in the wind, Zoltan handsome, erect, uniform spit-polished clean, make their way under the canopy of raised swords striding toward their loved ones taking the first important steps of their next 50 years together.

Maria + Zoltan

Hin und Zurueck (Over and Back)

Following the yellow brick road, slipping off to sleep, soft pillow, blond curls spreading out over the satin. Dreamland, diamonds glinting off the green tree branches; strawberries sprouting off bushes, plump over-red bursting with flavor.

A scent, a flavor drawing you down that road, an adventure to be taken, distortion, queens, kings, royal garb in a glass box looking out but not being able to touch. A flying purple horse overhead with a Walkuere in fuchsia feathered helmet astride bearing a banner welcoming sign to the wonderland of sleep. Follow the signs, the associations, the sunlight enveloping the valley with its rays, intense, over bright, golden rays turning to icy pitchforks, once gold, now silver, finally gun-metal ... 24 hours passing in the valley, the world turning swiftly below, lost time, spent time, gray time, blue time.

Dark valley, banshees swooping overhead, the vibration of their wings making the pavement ripple like too much sun, driving you to the castle, over the moat, past the peasants, into the courtyard, accompanied by guards in mail on grand Clydesdale horses. Marched into court before the King and Queen; she looking darkly down, he ineffective and passive shrugging his shoulders – she gesturing with her hand slicing across her throat, the guards lunge..... Lions, tigers and bears, oh my, oh my, oh my, oh my..........

Pressure on my forehead. I start abruptly to see mother standing over me.... A happy sigh....

Pas de Deux

Quiet Hush, blue background, grand gold proscenium arch
Corps de ballet lined up either side, lights dim
Bill and Susie, tomorrow's Nuryev and Fontaine
Pad quietly from the wings upstage, grand somber entrance
She in cloud blue gossamer, he in courtly white jacket with braded epaulet

A moment to poise, time stops, audience anticipation
They move a focused diagonal, he all graceful deportment,
She gliding as if on air, the pair circles, meets, passes, pirouettes
His grande jete inspiring gasps, her full-blown leap, a visual thrill upwards
Landing elegantly in his arms – arms of steel without so much as a quiver of effort. Parading with her overhead extended like a glorious bird until the music's cue brings them to earth

They promenade toward each other, another endless pirouette
Ending in the final breath-taking tableaux

Garter Snake

Green grass, sunny day, shadows cast by the chestnut tree,
Nothing apparent, yet unseen
A sleek young snake quietly slithers along the ground,
Slowly, steadily making his way
Into the sunlight

Beautiful elegant miniature serpent with orange eyes
Emerald skin gilded with fine gold scales
Rippling in the sunlight, subtle, sinuous movement
To the flat stone warm and welcoming your sunbath

You cannot linger on the stone, or you will become
An adult's threat or a child's treasure
You roll in the sun, absorb the stone's warmth, and then
Exquisitely slither away to the safety of the bushes
Away from the eyes of humankind

Dirge Familiare

Trudge, trudge, trudge, quietly, steadily, caisson ahead,
Troops behind, black riderless horse at the lead
Overwhelming respect, remembrance of a profound event,

A quiet serene moment of repose in the midst of
An army of mourners, a sweet old memory of a tune
As a counterpoint to the gravity

A wag conjuring up the feel of a French Romantic master
While attributing the tune to a famous Viennese songwriter
What would the new French music be without old Europe to rest on?

Cheetah Hopscotch

Galloping, galloping, faster faster,

Gazelle running flat out before,

Cheetah spots flashing behind

Pursuit........ Hurry....... Hurry .... Prey – oh my.

Cheetah transforms to Billy, lean, skinned knees

Chalk in hand frantically drawing a grid in the earth,

Will you play? Throw the chalk,

One foot, hop, hop, skip, oops, you hit a line

Balance, grab the chalk

Faster, faster, Jane, the Gazelle next in line....

Who will win?

Run, leap for joy..... prey's gone.......

What's this?

The end. Naw, really? Sure enough.... The end......

Fine, das Ende, Kaput, Fines, Adieu, Adios, Addio

Done, finish, totally? Yep

!!!!!THE END!!!!!

Beauty

Beauty, yes I have

The nicety of exterior that the masses rate you by,

That guarantee of things made easy for you. – if you only surrender the 'you'ness that is uniquely yours.

An automated doll, you wind up in the morning to go all day – keeping up a pristine Gestalt,

Beauty is expensive to the possessor, wrenching from the individual her normalcy, distorting even the simplest of relationships, robbing her of harmony, balance and calm.

Envied by all who see only the shell of a multi-faceted, rich personality that is suffocating for the fresh air that the plainer masses breath so easily, so unaffectedly,

Forced into the life of an outcast Pariah who roams the earth's surface like a blanked -out automaton, - the façade that one writhes behind in in quiet desperation.

Affair

No one ever decides to have an affair. Somehow that set of circumstances gets thrust on one unexpectedly. On no particularly significant day you are going about your business as usual and an arresting pair of eyes notice you and somehow you know the day will be very special. You exchange pleasantries, a prolonged look and go on your way. Yet, as the day passes, your attention keeps reverting back to that small fragment of time.

More days pass, life goes on. Until suddenly you meet those eyes again and you know this time more must be said. You search for something to say and yet you know there is danger there, for both of you. Abstain, ignore, it will disappear – wrong. It becomes bigger. Many sleepless nights pass until you realize you must follow your instincts or have no peace. Coincidental vignettes pop up in your mind. It must look casual, but interested. Several days you search for those eyes, half fearing their appearance, disappointed in their absence, until suddenly the meeting occurs face to face. Time stops, nausea surfaces - vulnerability. You stand there, naked with your instincts and he with his. Polite parlor talk begins, everyone is looking or so it seems. Terrible, frightening and wonderful; so it is to be human. Somehow you survive the first minutes until you realize your interest is returned. "Can I buy you a drink,?" "Certainly, I have a little time." The verbal sparring match continues for a couple of hours, until you think tonight? So soon, yet, have those eyes been out of your thoughts frequently those many nights? "Will he like me? Will I please him?" Certainly biology should take care of everything, but yet, will it? You want more than these few hours. And somehow mere humanness is not enough. Not for those eyes. The time is magical. As you near home you think, "The sink's full of dishes the house is a mess, the bed's not made!" He talks a blue steak, non-stop, nerves taut. The key turns in the lock. Life has changed since this morning – drastically. Will you survive the suffocating feeling? The bed is rolled back. Belts, zippers, buttons are fumbled with to distraction. Time stops again. As he kisses you good night – will he be back?

The next day euphoria dominates. The air is sweet, skies are cloudless, work is effortless. In the evening you return home alone; quite alone. Will he call you? More time passes, days and days. Were you fresh enough? Beautiful enough? Young enough? Those eyes so appealing to you are equally appealing to the rest of the feminine population. You are not so special – unique. The sex was rough, intense and not as expert as you have previously exhibited. Two and a half years alone; you're out of step, tired, depleted. Will he call?

You must see those eyes, yet are you strong enough to take rejection? Can you search him out? He has wife, family, prominent position. You cannot expose yourself or him. Both are vulnerable. Time will tell if you represent one of his not infrequent one-night-stands or – if he looked further beyond – to see you behind your eyes. You both have agreed "no strings" yet both have committed far beyond that already.

He calls. Where can he reach your more easily? Can you be more accessible? Inadvertently he tells you how long he is at the office after hours. Was it inadvertent? So innocent? Or, does he want you to call? Should you call? Or, stand on ceremony and provide, and wait for his next call? Age and insecurity hold you back. It is a man's world; you a mere, not so young woman.

One more week goes by, and you have your answer. "Would you like a ride home?" Suddenly age drops away and your vulnerability suddenly feels very good – exposed. You fly to meet him. Conversation is more direct – "no strings" – no strings – really? The night lasts forever, everything is mellow, beautiful, tender. The loving, the caring, bittersweet, sensuous, voluptuous. Total mutual giving. The phone rings – suspicion in those eyes – wrong number. And the warning, "Be careful how you handle strange calls." And yet, "no strings". The sensations last for days, until the next time. When? How long?

Sex

Man's magnetic center, intangible, radiating, gravitating,

Utter pit of humanness, embarrassment. Piquant;

Not beauty of face or form, but thought and mystery.

Propelling energy – mankind's ultimate

Achille's Heel.

The Executive

The man that most fear, or are intimidated by,

The one who throws his voice and by screaming at others drives them into silence so nothing more can be created, but only destroyed

The man who has spent his lifetime totally separate from his family to gain what... prestige... who is in a field that holds no love for him....

The man who simply got ahead by dotting his "i's" better than the others, who put in hours of mind-numbing work which was entirely useless to anyone save your higher executive who will get his pleasure from you by watching you lurch after a bit of idiocy...

What, you do it for? Money you say?, What, you have sold the major portion of your life in pursuit of what... the right to be called Mr. Executive Vice President...

Sure you need stroking now and then, but have you not sacrificed your very essence for the meager stroke (and I mean singular) from your "immediate superior" executive... WHY?

If you loved what you do, there would be real worth in the doing of it, but to sell yourself to a corporation, cock, balls and ass for one stroke that will come due 20 years from now. . . Where is that intelligence you so assiduously tout to all below you?

What you represent to your underlings is a bag of gaseous fumes that cannot be released even to your own satisfaction.

Yes, you intimidate your underlings but they only realize how powerless you are. You have no balls, no cock—you're simply a mindless extension of your higher-up who can very quickly and easily prick your bag and destroy you. If only your underlings knew how large a sham and bully you really are; if they would have the temerity to mutiny in the face of their own sold-out position. . . Yes, you rot at the core like an over-ripe peach that has blackened.

Someday, on your death-bed, you will look back and finally realize that you sold your soul for potential that never satisfied you and in so doing, LOST the very uniqueness that gives you your identity. You are a faceless blob pf protoplasm. . . .

That is all – 'you EXECUTIVE'!

Storm

The bowels of heaven issue forth the their black bolts of rage, impinging on the shell of the earth, massive,

Such power covers man, each infinitesimal second of life _ never venting itself, save for raining on the parched waiting earth,

Sweeping the chaff and waters in its way, brushing us with it into its heart–

This connection, regenerating our senses like a depleted cell . . . the power, the might of this energy.

Be swept away into its eye and lifted to the heights of our humanness at the whim of this glorious charger – this steed of the nighttime, the cool wind on your face as you plunge into blackness.

Human Nature in the Corporate Structure

To be me is not to be manipulated. I am nothing more than what I am, - 33 years worth of layers is what I am. I am alone, most times, happily so. But it is often that other people choose to inflict themselves on my life and interfere in the living of it. Complicated individuals are so disposed to their privacy that in their pursuit of it, draw people to themselves, thus thwarting their main goal – self discovery. Such is the nature of the beast.

The pursuit of the "big deal" seems to drive mankind. The majority of people jump to this beat. They knock their heads against the wall for the duration of their lives to the age of 65, all the while not fully realizing that a few "big " people pull the strings that the masses jump to. They feel they have put in their time and little realize that they have been used. When retirement comes or – "the big payoff", there is nothing , - the corporate structure will seek the easiest, cheapest and least responsible way out. John Q. Public is most certainly expendable. And just think, all the people you've screwed getting just that little bit ahead of all the others. Now is your turn to pay your karmic dues. "Gotcha"

That type of rat race is not me. I just want enough financial backing to insulate myself form life's many attacks, enough money to continue my search and fulfill my destiny. I am one of the fortunate ones. I know that I was put on this earth for. However, pursuing this destiny must be done the proper way . . . with the flow of natural development, savoring each turn of events as it surfaces. I could no more feel joy in reaching my goal at the expense of someone else than in clubbing someone to death. I guess the cleanest description I can come up with is ethics. All I ask is that I keep nonessential, neurotic and prohibitive people away. The simplest way is the best. That's the bottom line.

Mobility is really the key to survival. That and flexibility. To survive, you must always think of your enemy's weakest point. Everyone has an Achille's Heel. Don't ever forget it. To go on your way, you must deal with people, - friends, enemies and mere acquaintances. The last category and the first are the most dangerous. An enemy, in the normal course of things, is automatically mistrusted. Not so with a friend or acquaintance. That particular relationship can lull itself along with narry a ripple 'til one day you realize that by simply doing your job you have intimidated their security. Their sloth, ineptitude and general naivete have left them open to attack. Because you are strong and seemingly impervious, you are likely to become the focus of misplaced blame. It's always easy to pass the buck. And when we return to that infamous bottom line, the reply will always be, "better you than me". Just like Orwell's hero in 1984, "do it to Julia". This is the lowest essence of the human condition. The stronger an individual's character the longer it will take to break him down to his Achille's Heel. We all have that very basic Achille's Heel. That is man's common heritage. I'm not inviting you to aggressively mistrust people for this. Our purpose in life is to pursue our destiny. Nothing more – nothing less. Simply be aware of that Achille's Heel; know it exists there in every normal human being. And know, more importantly, that everyone will crumble at some point or another. It adds one more variable to the game of life.

I am not totally a pessimist. The human spirit, though weak, can be dauntless. I believe in it. Fate never forces all of us at the same time to that point of breaking. Thank God! As a result, the general cushion and flow of spirit carries our civilization forward most times, and to great heights less frequently. That is our hope for peace in this world. That is why the key to survival and a certain amount of happiness is flexibility and mobility – a lesson I learned very early in life.

Another variable that cannot be ignored is what we hold dear in life. If it happens to be an idea – that is good. It gives you the mobility that can raise the level of a culture or submerge it completely, if the person happens to be a dictator. And better still, if the individual with the idea has a concept of his particular function within the farm of society, then we have a valuable member of the team of life. The purpose - inherent in such individuals, is what raises a civilization to a culture, with much beauty for everyone.

This person is truly free and cannot be manipulated and hence is much less a threat to the rest of John Q. Public who simply wants to get on with his own pursuit of destiny.

However, no culture is so fortunate as to have the majority of individuals pursing their destiny with a major love of ideas. The majority of civilization is pushed forward (?!) by individuals who hold "things" dear. To our material society they are the "go-getters", highly productive individuals in a material sense; they are also most frequently the users and abusers of people and ideals – they crush the more tender-hearted and mystical creatures. Eventually they do chalk up enough black marks on their record so they receive a bit of a backlash from individuals in their way who have enough money or prestige to say, "NO" to them. That is when you see how quickly their Achille's Heel surfaces. They have few, if any emotional resources and precious little strength of character – so they crumble quickly. They are more vulnerable to attack than those who hold ideas dear. They have more, financially, to protect. That is why John Q. Public is so expendable to them.

I believe that the key to surviving the political corporate structure is to develop all your personal human capacities, so that one is rich enough personally to look at the corporation from a distance and keep perspective intact. Difficult – in that each person involved in the structure has his own ends to meet and satisfy; unfortunately the lack of love for what they do makes their motivation money. And then, when is enough money enough? Rockefeller was asked once how much money would be enough. And he replied that "just a little bit more" would be enough. So the question is age-old. Again we are talking about the individual who holds "things" dear.

Still it comes down to the fact that you have to please yourself in whatever you do. And when you don't please yourself, you're no good to anyone. Maybe there is no final solution to "Human Nature in the Corporate Structure" except to rethink and assess your values as an individual.

Ultimately the goal is not the important thing. It's the journey to the goal that is.

It is no good either to sit in one's Ivory Tower and pontificate; things improve, develop and gain that richness that we all need inside from the doing. You can't sit on the periphery. Corporations allow most people to sit on the periphery for very little reward indeed, but they do survive there, and that is the American Way. Is it so good to survive physically while the soul rots inside?

Alone at Midnight

The day has been usual, calm, routine. Instead of heavily driven productivity, the time passed in social discourse. You get home after an uneventful train ride and settle into your evening routine, placidly let the TV determine your evening. Calmly and benignly you end your day with the twist of the dial, put the lights out and pull the covers around you.

You doze for awhile only to see the luminous hands of the clock on the night stand. What was it that caught a fragment of your attention? Bit by bit the shadows disappear and the segments of idea connect and project clearly out of the darkness. That phone call earlier – what was the precise phrase which earlier had no malice, but now commands all of your attention? What terrifies so? The thought, or the hour in which you see it in bold relief? You readjust your covers and settle in again to the prospect of sleep. No luck – that fragment suddenly develops sharp edges that dig into your consciousness. Each time you turn over for sleep, it jabs you, just like a stone in your shoe. Suddenly, that problem which began minutes ago as a small localized ray, broadens out into a huge brilliant beam, not to be ignored. Somehow, try as you will, you mentally note one solution, - no good! Try another approach, - still no good. It's like a mountain that's too steep and slippery, with no toe-holds in sight to step into and hold on to. Just like the childhood nightmare of being chased by an unknown and unmentionable terror. There must be a way out, an escape to the problem. Even the most logical and obvious solutions don't appear practical or within the realm of possibility. Finally, all immediate thought of sleep evaporates. Perhaps the problem may not loom so large and insurmountable with the light on.

You flip the switch. The problem is still there and you are still definitely alone with it, but the broadness of its beam is less frightening now.

Can you cope with your thoughts, or is the prospect of ANY solution paralyzing. Your cat blinks at you curiously. If only he could talk. He could at last commiserate, if not resolve your worry. He readjusts his position, yawns and goes back to sleep. It would be nice if you could turn a switch in your head that would destroy the supreme concentration that normally evades control in the daylight, but now exerts such a strong magnetism. "I'm a normal, rational woman. This is childish." But, a child has a mother or father to call to in the night when the "bogey-man" takes over his sleeping hours. Not so now. That childlike innocence is still in evidence (or you wouldn't be wide at at 12 a.m.), but no one is there to cry to. Not even a lover to hold you. You are alone in the marauding world, especially so at 12 a.m. this night. Funny, how vulnerable we are. There is always a soft spot under our waking, people-confronting shell. Our own particular life experience determines at which point on our underside that that particular stone can cut through our softness, our weakness.

All would be easier if someone were there. That child in us is keeping us awake this evening. Somehow we must solve even a tiny portion of that gnawing problem immediately, without delay. We may not survive the night to rationally face that beam! Right now that beam is blinding any reasonable approach. All is bleak and hopeless at midnight . . . . .Alone.

The Other End of the Rainbow (the enchanted toilet)

"No, Rosa, I really want this apartment. But you must know that I have a cate, and if that is a problem, I want you to tell me that up front. I will never give up Oscar. He's my baby. We've been together since he was a kitten." With a shrug of her shoulders and a questioning look in her eyes: "Cat? Me speaka little English. Cat? Come se dice?" Dolly quickly translated: "Il Ghatto". "Ah, si Il ghatto, si . . . . " On those words, I just realized that I had placed a substantial amount of the money I saved for my move to New York on the line.

The apartment was modest, ¾'s of it below ground, quite dark, but with enough small basement windows to compensate. There were some strange red marks on the floor and three evenly placed soot marks on the wall of what was to become my bedroom. The place needed a paint job. If you overlooked the hole in the wall and the patched tiles on the floor as you stepped down into the bathroom, it really wasn't all that bad. I could afford it. The energetic bundle of red fur tinged with black snapping viciously at my window, added the last touch of security I so sorely needed on this my first month in New York. Safety was a determining factor in my choosing this apartment. Any apartment choice in New York is fearfully made, especially wen you live alone. My choice made, I could finally allow the realization to sink in – 1978 – I finally made it the culmination of the last 2 years near nervous breakdown and ensuing struggle to re-order my life.

The apartment was bare, expectantly awaiting the arrival of my belongings which were still in Wisconsin. Up until their arrival, Oscar and

I would have to rough it on a lone sleeping bag in the middle of my not-so-clean floor.

Our first evening alone together, after having scrounged up a few meager utensils form Woolworth's, Oscar and I had our first meal. Less than one week later, our belongings would arrive – actually, my belongings were the only things that verified my existence in this enormous impersonal town. Exhausted, we finally settle down to sleep. After shutting off my hearing to the street noise outside; the kids playing stick ball, with their ghetto busters turned up full blast, all that remained audible to my sense was the warm, small weight of Oscar on my feet, the occasional crunching of the cockroaches as they scurried across the floor and the slow drip of my bathroom faucet.

After two hours of sleep, something caught my attention – the curious glug-glug-glug of my bathroom drain. Just the neighbors flushing their toilet overhead. I quickly covered up again, settled Oscar back and dozed on through the night.

After my belongings arrived, the apartment became quite comfortable for the two of us. There was enough space to stretch out in, even though there was a rather dank odor to the surroundings.

Rosa had a husband whose eyes were always on some passing skirt, and two children, a boy and a girl – both with large dark liquid eyes; only the eyes of Italians have that luminosity. Many nights were punctuated by the running of children and dog feet overhead; joyous running, happy noises as only a close family can make. Bruno, as was his habit left 1 hour after their evening meal to join the other Italians in the café on Steinway Street. There they would talk the usual men-talk of the Italians.

Rosa would spend the evening occasionally in the company of Dolly, the woman who introduced me to Rosa and my apartment. Dolly was a fiftyish dish-water-blonde, who smoked too much, wore too much rouge and despite her Italian heritage, spoke in a rough Brooklyneese. I initially took her for one of the many shop clerks in the various small department stores in Queens, but actually, her husband had died 8 years before and she lived modestly on the income from a small pension he had set up for her. Dolly was cheerful, gregarious, slender, almost wraithlike, with heavy shadows under her eyes. She looked as though she had lived her 50 years and then some. But yet, she was an altogether pleasant woman, whose infectious humor took over any room she entered.

When I first moved into the apartment, Dolly was welcome and frequent company for Rosa and the kids. After awhile, I simply didn't see the woman any more. She lived right next door to us, but yet we never seemed to bump into each other as before. I knew she liked men, especially "New York's Finest", but she was decidedly discreet in her extra-curricular activities.

Before I digress too far, other than Dolly's company, Rosa would usually wile away the evening sewing for the kids or mindlessly watching the television that she didn't understand, probably hoping to pick up some English in the bargain. These were the many quiet nights lasting on into midnight when Bruno would return and give Rosa hear usual sound thumping in the bed overhead of my bedroom. How Rosa could really ever find Bruno attractive was quite beyond me. He reminded me of an orangutan, only not as intelligent looking, nor with the redeeming cuddliness of the ape. Altogether, as repulsive as I found Bruno, Rosa and the children were very very dear. They accepted me as a rather eccentric extension of their family, somewhat like an old maiden aunt, complete with her cat. I entertained few, if any friends, practiced my arias daily, painted and sewed for relaxation on the weekend. Rosa could always relate to the music, and frequently asked for the Schubert "Ave Maria", which I would gladly render through the tissue thin ceiling.

When I first moved in, I shared the company of that family many weekends on Sunday. And during the week, I helped the kids with their school work. Rosa and Bruno didn't understand, read or write English enough to help the kids, so I was their built-in tutor.

Life went on very comfortably for about eight months, when one night after work I arrived in my apartment around 6:00 p.m. to be greeted by a startled looking cat. The floor to my walkway was wet with a small amount of water. As I walked through my bedroom and turned into my bathroom, I sloshed through about two inches of water, - quite wet, quite filthy, complete with the green algae that you find in a backed up sewer. I sloshed further into the bathroom and looked into the shower stall. More of the brown molten liquid was oozing up from the sewer. I did as all normal females do. I immediately dialed up the landlord: "Ricky, get your father. My apartment is flooding." "I'm sorry, my father is at the restaurant." "Ricky, the water is coming in fast. I don't know what to do." "I'll run up to the corner and see if I can find him. " By this time, Rosa and Lucia were at my door looking down into the mess. "So sorry, your apartment. So much trouble . . . My husband a come right away."

The water miraculously abated some. At least it didn't get any higher. It filled my bathroom. Oscar, Rosa, Lucia and I looked on helpless as Oscar's litter box floated by on the filth. 45 minutes elapsed and Bruno, along with Ricky appeared on my doorstep. He and Ricky disappeared into the blackness of a closet in the hallway. I heard some banging and scraping, and then a woosh of water. Then quite suddenly as it had appeared the water suddenly seeped away steadily. "My husband and I will help you clean up." The three of us, with Oscar and the kids watching, mopped up the mess, scooping and sweeping the debris with the water back down in to the drain, where it had come from. As the family left to go back upstairs, Rosa turned and said, "Sues – so sorry for all the trouble." "I understand Rosa. I'm just grateful you came so fast. I've never had anything like this happen before. I don't know what I would have done without you."

Oscar and I were alone once again. I quickly cleaned up the mess that the family had left. Exhausted from our night's adventure, Oscar and I finally settled in to get some sleep.

Two months elapsed without incident. Oscar and I had settled into a nice routine. We would rise early at 5:30 a.m. and begin our day On one such work day, I went to the bathroom to use the john. I lifted the lid and to my horror was confronted with a sewer rat glaring balefully up at me. Stifling my scream, I immediately dropped the lid of the commode and flushed several times, hoping that the rodent would disappear. Fearing that he hadn't been flushed away, but yet unable to contain my curiosity, I lifted the lid once more. The bowl was empty, save a decent level of water. I shudder to think of what would have happened had Oscar discovered our guest before I did. The thought of the filthy creature running through my apartment with Oscar on its heels gave me goose flesh.

Once again, "Rosa, you'll never guess what I found in the toilet." "Rats – what do you mean – rats. We have never had rats. Do you still have it?" (As if I would have kept it as a pet!) "I'll send my husband down to look, but he has to go to work. Can it wait until tonight?" That evening, Bruno came down to inspect the plumbing. He banged on a few more pipes, grunted some and shook his head. "Are you sure you saw a rat? Maybe a mouse. We never had rats." Maybe you were dreaming?" After he left, still not feeling much better than before, and quite shaky to boot, Oscar and I sat down to eat, the thought of rats gnawing at my mind. Oscar was quite oblivious to my anxiety as he ate his cat food.

The days rolled by. Christmas came and went, New Years, and hard bitter winter. If you can call it hard or bitter in New York. Hardly anything to compare to Wisconsin's near arctic conditions. Finally, spring presented itself in all its freshness. Central Park was pink with the blossoms on the trees and the odor of grass growing in the humid ground mixed with the fragrance of the blooms permeated the air. With all this growth came the usual spring rains which of course overloaded the sewers.

Miraculously through all of this, my apartment stayed dry. You could have slept on the bathroom floor through all of it, even though the drains would periodically glug-glug merrily away, giving me anxiety attacks.

One evening, I woke up out of a sound sleep to an enormous crash of water. You rememeber the line, "Water, water everywhere and not a drop to drink". That's what first raced through my mind. However, those words were inspired by someone with an incredible thirst. My association was based on the fear of suddenly drowning in my sleep with Oscar scrambling for those basement windows. In the blackness of my bedroom, I heard voices: "What, It couldn't have happened. Oh mio Dio! We'll have to shut the water off. I wonder if Sues is awake. I hope the drain takes it all. We won't have any water tomorrow." Along with this dialogue I could hear the sloshing of water on the other side of the furnace room wall. My first thought, "my piano. Water will ruin it. I may as well throw it out completely. I'll never be able to afford replacing it." Figuring nothing could be done, and that things had probably gotten as bad as they could, I rolled over and slept through til morning. Oscar, after pacing back and forth a bit settled in for the rest of the night.

Morning came. I went to the bathroom as usual to draw water from the faucet. Nothing. Just rust and spurts of air greeted my attempts. Then I remembered. No water. Some section of the apartment was under water again. I went to the practice room to see how my piano was. Although I could hear the water lapping at the other side of the furnace room wall, the floor beneath my piano was dry. The entire apartment had been spared. I still couldn't draw water, but I realized eventually I would have water, however, in the meant time, I had to get to work, and I could not very well go to work with a night's worth of cold sweat on my body. I called Bruno.

"Bruno, I don't have water, - not event hot water. I need to bathe. What do I do"?" "didn't you hear anything last night. The boiler broke. All we have is cold water and we have to turn that on from downstairs manually." "I need to go to work. I smell. "Could I have at least 5 gallons?" Grudgingly, they turned on the water. It was rusty. I bathed. "Can't you wash a little faster. We want to get some sleep." After finishing my ablutions, I turned on my hairdryer to blow myself dry. At least it was warm.

As I walked to the subway, I reflected on the past night's events. How could I have misjudged my surroundings so? Everything looked innocuous when I moved in. My private, safe little home, my peace of mind all shattered because God knows what will happen next with the plumbing. It's as if the plumbing had a mind of its own. No matter what I do, nothing works and sporadically so that I could go for months without incident and yet....

The summer months came with high humidity and temperature in the 90's that lasted for days. There was no respite from the heat. The kids opened up the fire hydrants and let the water run freely, dowsing anyone who passed by from head to foot. Long, hazy days in which most of the New Yorkers spent their evenings sitting on the stoops, only to retire late in the evening and sweat the night through. I heard very little thumping through these months.

The last days of summer arrived with fall pursuing on its heels. We had a wonderful warm fall with an October high in temperature and humidity. I had been out for the weekend only to return Sunday night. I heard the row going as I hit he door, "You didn't. How could you? In front of the children?" "Rosa, I love you. She really didn't mean anything to me. Just a flirtation. You were off with your sister the last couple of days and then you were too tired when you came to bed. What was I supposed to do? I have rights too." "Quiet, Sues just came in. She'll hear us." Their conversation sounded ominous. My command of Italian covered only the canzonettas and arias I sang. And of course, when my name was mentioned, my first thought, "what did I do now?" As suddenly as the voices began they subsided. I went downstairs to settle in for the night. Everything was quiet and uneventful.

Morning came. It was a beautiful day, bright clear, pleasantly cool in its break from the previous week's stoked furnace. And I had the entire Monday to myself. Fittingly enough, Columbus Day. My friend, Phyllis and I had decided to go biking into the city. The family above had all left to attend the parade in town. The house was empty, save for Oscar and me. I had just finished the dishes and picked up the house, when I heard a glug-glug from the bathroom. That noise made me decidedly edgey. I decided to check. Nothing amiss. Suddenly, another glug-glug from the kitchen sink. I rushed back and to my horror the sink was belching up a black putrulescent liquid. At this very moment, I heard a loud sloshing noise and ran back to the bathroom, Oscar fast at my heels. More of he black stuff came oozing out of the shower drain. Suddenly – a knock at my door. I nearly screamed. Phyllis was there. "What's the matter?" "The plumbing is going crazy . . . the sink in the kitchen, the bathroom . . . I don't know what to do, and everyone is gone. I have simply had it; and a plumber won't get here fast enough. I'm going to try to fix it myself. Will you stand by if this thing explodes on me? Whenever Bruno repairs it he goes to the closet and I hear a scraping, banging noise. Let's see what's in the closet." I opened the closet door and on the floor there was a round wooden platform. I tipped it on its side and rolled it into the corner. Beneath it were two very large metal plugs. A large pipe wrench was placed strategically across both of them. I lifted the heavy wrench and tried one of the plugs with it. It didn't fit, and no matter how small I turned the setting, it still would not fit either one of the plugs. With the glug-glug of the shower drain pounding in my ears, I decided on a desperate move. There was a large bricklayer's hammer laying in the corner of the closet. I picked it up and lightly tapped the edge of one of the plugs. Phyllis and I held our breath. It gave way and its contents exploded with human feces, matted up toilet paper, a milky odoriferous liquid, not to mention green algae that apparently had been clinging to the side of some pipe wall. After I recovered from my revulsion, I plunged my hand into what had previously been a clear opening. In the trap I found a small bar of soap that had become lodged tightly. I removed it, and cleaned out the walls of the trap, and as suddenly as the episode started, the glug-glugging stopped, the house was quiet, and the water receded. Victoriously, I looked at Phyllis, "I fixed it myself. I don't have to bother Bruno anymore. I don't have to fear this damned bathroom. It's perfectly reasonable." Phyllis couldn't really share in my happiness, but was pleased anyway. We set about cleaning up after the mess. Once finished, out the door, to the parks and a wonderful day.

The day had been well spent. It was good to see my good friend Phyllis. Phyllis and I had been through many things together, and her recent move from an apartment to a duplex gave us many happy hours of planning her room arrangements, buying furnishings and above all, scheduling an open house that was to take place in a month. Of course, since Phyllis' main reason for moving to New York had been the acquisition of a husband, this party was most definitely on her mind and mine.

With that preoccupation and the reflection on a lovely day well spent, I retired after feeding Oscar. I slept fitfully, and in my dream . . . . I was in a yellow room with cables hanging off the wall. It was oppressive, dirty, and dank. As I tried to focus in closer on something in the corner of the room – a day-bed . . . a feminine voice, "You son-of-a-bitch. Don' you ever try that again. I'll get you." The force of those words broke my sleep completely. I woke up in a cold sweat, only to hear the loud ticking of my alarm clock on the night stand. I turned on the light to dispel the awful feeling. 3 a.m. Oscar, who had been sleeping on my legs looked up at me and yawned. I felt rather foolish for my fear, turned out the light, rolled over and tried to sleep.

The next day, I ran into Phyllis and she asked, "You look awful. What happened?" "Usually I sleep very well, but last night I had a nightmare. Anyway it seemed like one. I rarely remember them, but this one I can recall quite clearly." "You've been working too hard. You have to slow down." I accompanied Phyllis to the subway. The train was coming overhead; she ran for it, leaving me on the platform to wait for mine.

On Saturday, I decided to have my hair done. After having done my marketing and tidying up my house, I left the apartment. Three and a half hours elapsed. I left he apartment. Three and a half hours elapsed. I had my hair totally restyled and was quite pleased with my hairdresser's efforts. I picked up my mail and went downstairs. The walkway was wet. I opened the door to my apartment and was greeted with 2 inches of clean water. This time it smelled after clothes washing detergent. Perfectly clean. Oscar was standing on my bed looking in the direction of my bathroom. He didn't want to get his feet wet. The wastebasket and the throw rug were floating on the crest of the waves. His litterbox had been filled to the brim. I called Rosa, " the plumbing is backed up again, but I don't think it's the same thing this time. Somehow, the water came in from above." "my husband- a come right down." Minutes later, Bruno came clomping down the stairs. "See what I mean? Oscar's litterbox shouldn't have filled up if it had been the drain backing up." "I dunno Sues," as he turned on the faucets to the sink. A small amount of water seemed to come from the base of the sink, but not enough to mention. "See – I think that's our problem. The pipe connection that goes to the shower is leaking. I think that's it." "No Bruno, Oscar's litterbox shouldn't be full of water if that's the case. The water must have over flowed form the commode tank this time." "No Sues, if we replace the pipe, it should take care of it." Rosa looked on with those large soulful eyes and said, "so sorry Sues, all the time so much trouble, my husband will fix."

My Sunday was shot completely with sections of my shower wall getting ripped out to replace the pipe on the sink. I stayed at my piano and worked on my music; my quiet German lieder interrupted by the clank, thud and the noise of drilling. At 6:00 p.m. Bruno called m, "Sues, come look . . . I fixed it." He did all right, but there was still the gaping hole in the base of my shower wall to contend with. At least when I showered, it didn't leak back onto the bathroom floor. Well, something was better than nothing. Relieved, but still with the gnawing thought that nothing had really been fixed, I led Bruno out of the apartment.

That evening, at 11 p.m., as I was reading in bed, I heard the familiar glug-glug and then a woosh of water that sounded as though it was pouring down the sides of the wall. I jumped out of bed, and ran into the shower, Oscar right behind me. The water was backing up. I dialed Bruno's number: "Bruno, the water is coming in fast." "Can it wait until morning Sues?" "No, it's flooding my apartment," In the minute or two that I had been on the phone with Bruno, my entire bathroom floor was under water. I couldn't believe how fast, as though the damn sewer had a mind of its own. A few minutes later, I heard the clomp, clomp of Bruno's feet as he came down the stairs. He smelled faintly of liquor, clad only in a dirty t-shirt and trousers that hung beneath a prominent belly. "Whatsa matta Sues?" "Look at this mess. I thought you fixed it. I told you that it was something else. What's causing this to happened repeatedly?" "I dunno, let's see now . . . " as he went into the closet. I heard the usual clanking and scraping noises, and finally as though in one big motion, he must have pulled the plug . . . again the water disappeared into the drain. "Thatsa betta. You calla me any time, I'lm sorry it happened. I gotta get some sleep. Buona notte." "Buona notte."

I heard his footsteps overhead as he approached the bedroom. That's when the fight started. "What she want again? You spend all day down there and leave me alone. Can't you fix anything?" The battle raged on and only fleetingly did I understand the conversation. One a.m., finally in my bed, I fell asleep. In my dream: I was in the same yellow room with the light cables hanging from the wall. This time, I saw a very beautiful girl with long dark hair and huge black eyes. She was burning incense at a small altar with a strange looking figurine on it. Three black candles were lit in succession and her voice, "Chand-il-manhatie sobayaka rosh halatie. Hatna mesarmen dou jaladie, meskino raba . . . " The words didn't mean anything to me. But somehow, their cadence sounded familiar. I didn't like what I was seeing and suddenly I was roused from my sleep by Oscar's pawing at my cheek. He was terribly upset and I quickly understood why. The sink in the kitchen was glug-glugging merrily away. I jumped out of bed to investigate. The sink had a small geyser bubbling from it. The stuff was pitch black. I stood there transfixed. Then I heard the loud swooshing of water in the bathroom. I ran back to it, looked into the shower. Nothing.

This time, water was shooting from the commode. I couldn't believe my eyes. Terrified , I ran for the phone to call Bruno. The phone didn't answer. I ran up the stairs and banged on their door. They weren't home. Nearly hysterical, I called Phyllis and got her out of bed.

"What do you want? Do you realize it's three a.m.?" "Phyllis, help, I don't what's going on. I just woke out of a dream, and water is shooting out of the kitchen drain. I can't stop it and Bruno isn't home. He's spent the entire day fixing things here and nothing has helped, and now the commode is spraying water form under the tank lid." "Settle down, I'll be right over to get you. You can spend the night at my place. Bring Oscar along."

An hour passed, and Phyllis arrived at my door. She and I both went to the drain. There was no water. There weren't even any stains. Nothing. "Are you sure you haven't been drinking?" "No Phyllis, believe me, when I called you there was black water shooting out of the kitchen drain. Let's check the commode. If it flushes cleanly, then my drains should be alright." I tried the commode. Everything worked. "Your nerves are nearly shot, Sue. I'll stay with you the rest of the night. It's almost morning anyway." Then I told her about my dreams. I believe she thought that I might be near another breakdown. She knew about my near-miss in Wisconsin.

Two hours later, I got out of bed to start my day. Phyllis, who had spent the night on my sofa, was sleeping soundly. I needed to use the commode. When I flushed it, cold water spurted all over me from underneath the lid. Out of frustration, or sheer stupidity, I lifted the lid. I was getting soaked form head to foot. "Phyliss, for God's sake help me. This damn thing is going to flood the place. It won't shut off." Phyllis ran into the room. As Oscar watched us, Phyllis managed to put her hands over the strategic spots and stemmed the leak in the dike. It finally shut off. "See, it's nothing. Somebody jammed a rag over the shut-off valve, and it floated around and got stuck. We should be able to repair this very easily. Are you sure you really want to live here? You know you could come stay with me until you get something better". "No, I do feel safe here; I better check to see how much a good plumber will cost. I can't afford to move now. New York is simply too expensive."

Exhausted from the exertion, we both dragged ourselves back to bed.

Two p.m. the next day.

"Phyl, this plumbing -problem has taken up so much of my attention this last week, I forgot to buy groceries, and Oscar's out of food. Do you want to come along?" "Not really, I should go home and feed poor Sniff. She'll be hungry by now and probably has thought I have abandoned her, poor little bugger. But I'll walk part of the way with you." "She is a people cat, much like Oscar. But then Siamese are more frail than the larger breeds. I hope she'll be alright. She had to spend the night alone, thanks to me. I feel terrible for having involved you." "Hey – what are friends for?" After climbing out of my apartment and walking a couple of blocks in the sunlight, "Well, I'll call you tonight to see how you're doing. Take it easy now, OK?" "Yes Phyl, but thanks again so much for coming over last night."

I went into the grocery store, still quite upset and very tired, did my shopping and then stood in the check-out line - especially long at that hour of the day. While waiting, I ran into Dolly, "Well, where have you been? I haven't seen you in ages. How have you been?" "Sue, it's good to see you. I left the neighborhood, and moved to a new place." "Why?" Her face darkened, "My blasted landlord. He's a real bastard. I was able to afford my little place. I lived there for over 10 years. He got greedy, and decided to break the wall down separating the apartment next to mine from mine so he could charge a fancy rent for one large apartment. I couldn't afford the rent, so I had to leave." "That's terrible. I knew something must have happened. I hadn't seen you with Rosa in a long time." "I don't talk to Rosa and Bruno anymore." "What do you mean? I thought you liked them so much Dolly." "I did. But did you notice how he chases women?" "Ja, I guess. He's not the most appealing man, but then I'm not married to him, either. And frankly, I don't think anyone would be attracted to him." "Well Sue, he approached me one night when Rosa was in the next room. I told him to keep his filthy hands off of me . . . that I wouldn't have him, if he were the last man alive. Since then, Maria has stopped talking to me. He apparently told her something else. That whole family can go to hell. After all I've done for them." "I must tell you something, Dolly. Things have been off the wall the last few months." "Really? Why?" "I have had nothing but grief with my plumbing. My whole apartment has been a shambles. The sewer keeps backing up through every drain it can find. Nothing seems to work. Bruno comes down repeatedly to repair things, and no sooner does he repair something, then it breaks, and I have flooding from another section of my place. I love my place. Like you, I can afford it. I can't afford to relocate now. I don't know what I'm going to do. Did anybody before me have any problems?" "And how, - but not the kind you're describing." "What do you mean?" "He always seems to rent that place to young single girls. The man has a one-track mind." Why didn't you warn me about him when I accepted the place?" "I realized you couldn't afford much. And at the time, after what happened with the girl before you, I figured he'd leave you alone." "What happened to her?" "She was a good-looking Puerto Rican girl with long hair and big boobs. She was a very nice girl, but very streetwise . . . also a very nasty temper. She and the family got along very well, although she didn't help the kids like you do. I don't think her education was very good, but she was a nice person. They all got along very nicely, even to having Sunday dinners together. She lived there about a year and a half, and one night I heard a big row. Her boyfriend picked her up in the middle of the night. The following week, Bruno had moved all her stuff out into the streets. I ran into her about a month later. The son-of-a-bitch tried to rape her. Can you imagine that? Right in his own house? She moved in with her boyfriend. I can't say as I blame her. After that, I never saw her again." "Oh my God – and that's what I have living over my head! He hasn't tried anything on me though. Probably because Rosa and the kids and I are pretty close, plus I have bailed the kids out of a couple of tight spots at school. Maybe that's why. I still wish the plumbing would work. I can't even afford to get an outside plumber. I'm afraid if I start, the bill will be astronomical when he's finished. And yet, Bruno doesn't seem able to fix anything." "Good luck Sue. If I were you, I would move out. He's a real son-of-a-bitch, that one." "Well, it's been good seeing you Dolly. Take care of yourself." "You too Sue."

Interesting. I had never thought of Bruno in that light before. I saw that he noticed, but then a lot of men look, and do absolutely nothing about. it. Anyway, I had a lot of groceries to pack away, and so I hurried home. Oscar greeted me at the door, not with the usual bright hello . . . so he was pretty tired too. After the groceries, I spent the day watching the soaps while doing a little correspondence. In the evening I practice as usual. Ten p.m. I went to bed. What a day. I could not shut off all that had happened in the last 36 hours, and seeing Dolly again, didn't exactly calm my nerves. Finally, I slept.

In my dream, I saw the same dirty yellow walls with the light cables hanging loosely. And the girl again, very beautiful with long dark hair. The black candles were lit again, the incense burning . . . "Beda sade sada dina mine eik melek seih-sin maklub al-mergie." Then abruptly the scene changed. Now she was standing over the commode with something white with red stains in her hand. It suddently hit me. That was my bathroom and my bedroom, and as she held the loaded sanitary napkin over the opening to my commode, "Salah mak lub kwasa . . . " followed by, "and with these words, you will never be able to rent this apartment again. It ill be unfit for human habitation." She flushed the loaded sanitary napkin down the commode. It went smoothly with narry a glug-glug or ripple. I was dumfounded by this development. I came away with a sense of awe and continued to ruminate in my dream. Quite suddenly. . . . glug-glug-glug, gurgle, splash woosh. The dream seemed to be changing. It got noisier with a sudden grinding noise. The noise woke me up. I jumped out of bed and found myself standing ankle deep in water, not water, but raw sewage. The place was flooded. Oscar was howling at me from the window ledge above. The dream had held me in slumber past Oscar's attempts to rouse me from sleep. I sloshed my way through to the other end of my apartment, . . . the water was creeping up my piano legs, everything was slowly going under. I quickly threw on a coat, grabbed Oscar, my purse and ran for my phone. I dialed Bruno, no answer. I let it ring 10 times. With each ring the water level was rising. I gave up in panic. I called Phyllis. "Come and get me. My apartment is going under, the whole place is flooded. I'm knee deep in water." "It can't be, it's never gone that high before." Phyllis responded. "It has now and I know why . . . (the noise of the water rushing in my ears) . . . somebody put a curse on this place. I have to get out of this place fast. Please – will you come and get me?" "Of course I will, I'll come as fast as I can." With those words I heard a sudden crash as the wall separating the furnace room and boiler area came tumbling down over my piano making a chaotic musical racket.

Fearing that the remaining walls would give way I hurried for the steps. I ran up the steps, Oscar in my arms. He was shaking with fright, his eyes big as saucers as he looked at our Atlantis sinking beneath the sewers of New York. I banged on Bruno's door. No answer. I heard another crash as the boiler tipped over. More water. I ran out of the house. As I stood on the street listening to the noise still coming from the apartment, I realized Bruno and his family had already left. Homeless, Oscar and I waited for Phyllis.

Commuting in New York City Some Observations

The 59th Street Bridge is my favorite place to be. It is my practice room on the way to and from work. It is my castle in the sky and the atmosphere changes there every day depending on who is crossing, the number of bikers pushing through. It's the perfect place for New Yorkers to actually have some privacy, under the canopy of the skies above, more sociable in good weather and absolutely private in bad weather.

The spanning of the East River was dreamed of as early as 1838. Roebling initiated his first plans for the bridge in 1856. In 1902 Mayor Seth Low hired Gustav Lindenthal as commissioner of the new Department of Bridge, so the building of the current structure was finally underway. Building a bridge is no small task and frequently it is a learn-as-you-go process. In 1907, for the second time, a newly built section of the bridge collapsed. The bridge was completed in 1908 and on March 30, 1909 the bridge opened to the public at a cost of $20 million and 50 lives.

My initial exposure to the 59th Street Bridge was sudden and extreme. It was the late 1970's and the MTA workers went on strike. Anyone living outside the state could hardly imagine millions of out-of-shape New Yorkers huffing and puffing their way along the roadside, then up and over the slow, steady and exhausting incline of the Bridge during rush hour. But I was among the new émigrés – my own choice. I came to New York slender and athletic, and like anyone who had gone to college in the Midwest, I had been used to driving my trusty bicycle wherever I had to go, loaded down with a sturdy backpack *without* a helmet – red hair (or so it was then) blowing in the breeze. These were the days before helmet laws. The Transit Strike proved to be a 17-day lark for me, and a change of commute overall since I found my trusty three-speed actually faster than the R train. I could make it down to 2 Broadway from Astoria in a little under 55 minutes – the train – well that could be as fast as 55 minutes but usually slower and much more irritating.

The transit strike – yes – the out-of-shape New Yorkers in their fancy business suits, heavy briefcases, women in spike heels. They were amusing to watch. Many people car-pooled. I just rode my bicycle and watched everyone under their own personal duress. I didn't even notice the Bridge. When you commute back and forth to work on a bicycle, you are too busy staying alive and out of the way of crazy pedestrians, cabs, busses and other bikers to pay much attention to things around you. I ended up commuting 3 years on my bicycle. Then I changed jobs, got back on the R train and gained weight.

My next interlude with the 59th Street Bridge was brief – midst thousands of people trying to get out of Manhattan on **9/11**. I could not see the bridge for all the people and the blocked lanes. It was faster to walk and incoming traffic was prohibited. What I remember the most about that day is the smoke filled air and the breeze on the bridge periodically blowing it away so you could look down to the tip of Manhattan where there was a very clear, very large column of thick black smoke rising straight up in the air where the World Trade Center used to be. After **9/11** we all held our collective breaths hoping that New York City would survive economically and that our lives would not change too much.

I only fully made the acquaintance of the 59th Street Bridge in the last part of 2003. I moved to New York to find myself and to fully become myself as only artistic types can in this incredible city. I am a singer, a pianist, a painter, and hopefully with this modest book, a writer. I pay for my habit working as a legal secretary. Legal secretaries have to be sturdy enough to withstand *a lot of stress*. I generally am, but one day I finally hit the wall. And since I was out of shape, and since I did not want to take tranquilizers, I began to walk. I discovered the connection between physical activity and my peace of mind.

Each morning I leave my apartment at precisely 7:30 a.m. It takes me a half an hour to walk south on Crescent to the Bridge. It takes another half hour to walk the entire span of the Bridge, and then 10 minutes further south to my job (at which time I might cram in a fast visit to the Post Office or the neighborhood grocer). Since I am loaded down with music, lunch, big purse (what woman in New York does not have a big purse?), heavy coat and tennis shoes, I do not hurry. Rather, I walk very easily and steadily. I estimate the distance I cover in my morning walk over the Bridge to be roughly 4 miles.

The Bridge has been a solace and revelation to me. The pathway to the top of the arch of the Bridge is initially canopied on the Queens side with tremendous spidery steel architecture, intricate and inviting as you pass beneath. There is a point where you emerge from beneath the canopy where the air is very quiet. If you have been chilly before, this is where even in late fall you will loosen your jacket and take your scarf off. This is also the point at which the train descends from above and bisects the line of the Bridge walkway before it descends into the tunnel. From here you can look at the train and all the people on it. This is also the place where the train frequently stops and gets stuck for 10 minutes while an indecipherable announcement blasts or gurgles over the loudspeaker: "We are waiting for another train to pass from the other track. It will take a few minutes." This makes me grin. Six thousand people are for the moment stuck in a hot stifling train, with all the wackos, pick-pockets, panhandlers, the malodorous cooking preferences of the various nationalities evident in the perspiration and methane rising upwards in the sealed car. I am outside in the fresh air moving right along.

I digress for a moment. I remember one such train ride where an unfortunate turbaned fan of curry became the focus of abuse from another passenger. I felt for the poor man as the mink-clad woman yelled at him for breaking wind in the car in close quarters when no one could escape – how he should have held it – could have held it – and that the train now smelled of excrement. The poor man turned eggplant purple with embarrassment. I turned toward the window with my back to the pair as did many others in the car. Our sides collectively shook with the effort not to laugh. That's why when I see the train stopped on the tracks at this point, I grin. They say that when too many rats are crowded together they will attack and devour one another. Well the woman in the white mink coat certainly turned on the hapless man in the turban. But the odor was *awesome*.

After my stress in extremis – i.e. a really bad nightmare that left me hoarse for three weeks in the care of a throat specialist, I set out on my first walk over the bridge. It was raining lightly when I set out so I was clad in a light trench coat, scarf (sneakers on my feet) and carrying an umbrella. I made my way along Crescent. The closer I got to the Bridge, the more jammed up the traffic and the heavier the rain. I began to have second thoughts about my expedition, but vowing to avoid tranquilizers altogether I pushed on. I skirted a growing puddle of water at the base of the bridge. Who besides me would be mucking about in the rain on the Bridge? Actually, quite a few people. Once past the first intersection I began my ascent. It rained harder. The wind picked up. Two men on bicycles were riding toward me, one in the latest racing gear with a shiny new bike. The second on a very old Schwinn with big tires which had seen better days. The rider of this antique was wearing blue jeans, a grubby windbreaker, a reversed baseball cap and a black garbage bag tied over his shoulders, a hole punched through for his head – an impromptu poncho. It immediately occurred to me that the brakes on the expensive bike would not work in the rain and the Schwinn tires probably had no tread and would slip on the wet pavement. I moved to the right to let them pass. The north-side path on the Bridge is wider than most cars by 4 feet or better, so there's plenty of room. However, I have seen bike crashes in the rain, so better safe than sorry.

Safely past the two bikers, I gain altitude and realize that an umbrella is utterly useless on any elevated landmark. I do battle with my umbrella. It inverts and I close it to regain control. I wish silently that I had a garbage bag poncho to cover me. I was getting soaked. Another biker passes me from behind. It was a pleasant Korean woman dressed appropriately for the storm. Her bike has baskets full of supplies – no backpack. She has a very heavy looking chain wrapped around her waist, a helmet and a clear plastic poncho. She is dry. I am not. I thought she would pass me by and continue on over the bridge, but she stops for a moment, jumps off her bike, turns to me and says, "Good morning. I haven't seen you here before." I suddenly feel very positive and happy. Who said New Yorkers were cold and aloof? Her name is Janet and she commutes to work over the bridge every day. She suggested that I reconsider my rain gear for my next walk into town, remounted her bicycle and pedaled swiftly on her way.

This chance meeting with Janet set the tone for all my experiences on the 59th Street Bridge. I see Janet several times each week. Sometimes we talk, sometimes we say "hi" but she always brightens my day. It occurs to me that the fresh air and physical activity clear the cobwebs from my brain. This is a good thing.

Another Monday morning, I am late, getting out of the house by 7:38 a.m. – 8 minutes to make up. The air is crisp and clear and I make my way south on Crescent. Two blocks south I see a man feeding bread crumbs to the birds. In 2004 a $50 fine for feeding birds was instituted but what Scrooge would report the man? I judge him to be in his early 70's. He has a bag of bread crumbs for the pigeons. The pigeons are lined up like tin soldiers on the telephone wires overhead at the intersection waiting, and in a flurry of blue/grey they all descend on the bread crumbs crowding close to the man's legs. The mutual pleasure between the birds and man for a moment remind me of what is real. I grin and walk past – the man nods. Ten feet beyond I see a small pile of rice next to the parked cars in the bakery parking lot. The smaller more delicate birds are enjoying their breakfast there – the old man ever watchful to the contrast in appetites, size and aggressiveness in the common birds – birds that are generally thought a nuisance in New York.

It reminds me of the Red Hawk controversy on Fifth Avenue. Some bonafidedly wild hawks took residence on one of the fancier Fifth Avenue apartment buildings. Their nest was enthusiastically observed by birders, naturalists and just normal folk. PBS actually did a special on the hawks. Some New Yorkers were not pleased, particularly when the common pigeon was a major part of the Red Hawks' diet. Tenants of the building, Paula Sonn among them, sued to have the nest removed. They removed the nest, and her popularity plummeted, so they re-built a platform for the hawks to return to.

I'm with the old man. I think the pigeons are the most graceful beautiful birds physically and their flight pattern is particularly exhilarating. They are wild too, just not exotic.

Further down the way, I pass an old woman who is methodically sweeping and collecting trash along the sidewalk in front of the Assembly of God building. She does it every day, beginning around 7:30 a.m. I wonder if it's her contribution to the church. Perhaps she is too poor to tithe....., but I do see her every day on my way.

Beyond the church there are two middle schools to the left, one appears to be a general PS, the one closer to the Bridge, a parochial school. There are two very pleasant crossing guards on either end of the public school block. Since I walk daily, I have a friendly nodding "good morning" exchange with them. I'm not so sure I would want to be standing out there when it really gets bitter cold though.

When you walk regularly to work at the same time, you tend to see the same people. Eventually, you can gauge whether you are late or early by where you meet on the bridge. There is one very handsome man I meet consistently. He wears beige twill trousers and a short-sleeve white t-shirt and always an off-white baseball cap on his head – no sunglasses, but black rimmed glasses. When it rains, he carries an umbrella, when it's colder he dons a windbreaker, and in winter a much heavier jacket. He smiles readily and we consistently greet each other – over all he has a very bright positive presence. If I'm late, I meet him at the base of the bridge on the Queens side. If I'm on time I meet him just over the crest of the bridge near the top.

I was so taken with his appearance and demeanor that I did an acrylic painting of him. The ability to paint someone from memory is something I developed at the Art Students League. Of course I only painted my impression. A month later, when the weather was hot, I noticed him take his hat off to wipe his brow with a red bandana. He was quite bald – not that it made any real difference, he was still a very handsome man, but he was older. I guess hair or the lack of it does make an impression. A week later, really having no need for the painting, I rolled it up, affixed my business card – and got lucky. I met him, gave him the painting and told him to give it to his mother or his wife. That's when I caught the Spanish accent. The next day on the Bridge, he thanked me for the "beautiful" painting and said his wife really liked it. It made my day. However, the lesson for me was that each of us is much more than our appearance, and talking animatedly with someone is definitely an enriching experience.

There is another fellow on the bridge. I meet him roughly at the crest of the bridge each day. He is roughly 6 feet tall, balding, reddish hair, blue eyes, glasses, broad forehead. He has an assertive no-nonsense stride. In colder weather, he wears an expensive jogging suit. In hot weather, good trousers and a teal colored knit shirt (soaked through with perspiration). His clothes are expensive. On his back he carries a heavy backpack. He always wears a big set of noise canceling earphones – he looks vaguely like an alien from outer space. In his hands he is carrying a currently published hard-bound book – not a library copy – and he is reading intently as he walks. I might do the same, but on a four mile walk, my book would be a paperback. I imagine how heavy that book must get by the time he arrives at his destination. He appears to read roughly a book a week in his commute. I wonder if he ever breaks out of his silence to notice anything around him.

It's taken several months, but he and I now wave at one another and just last week he shared his walk with a dark haired man in a business suit and top coat – judging from the pair's posture and verbal interplay, I surmise that the man with the alien was a foreign associate who had come to New York on business – I picked up an odd German phrase as I met them - that day the alien only nodded my way as he passed.

Now it's getting too cold. The alien no longer reads his book. He is wearing earmuffs, a hat and scarf and has his hands jammed in the pockets of his much heavier coat, but now he says "hi" out loud as we pass. I'm quite sure when it's really bitter, I will be alone on the bridge. The alien will know better than to trudge out in inclement weather.

Halfway out over the water as you look down to the right you see Roosevelt Island. *I paraphrase a Wikipedia entry of years ago,* "The first Dutch owners knew it as Hogs Island – later purchased by the Blackwell family. Originally there were active mined quarries on the island. In 1828, New

York City purchased the island for $32,500. A large penitentiary stood on the southern tip of the island.

The octagonal ruin at the northern end of the island and below Coler Hospital is the only reminder of America's first "Municipal Lunatic Asylum" (1839). It was visited by Charles Dickens in 1841, who commented on its magnificent staircase, its woe-be-gone inmates and the tourists flocking to see both.

A lighthouse (constructed in 1874) overlooks the swirling Hellgate waters, and according to a Renwick Design, was preceded by long "negotiations" with John McCarthy, an asylum inmate who'd built his own clay fort there to defend against British invasion. Until the 1960's Maxey's (Mc Carthy's nickname) crudely carved plaque could be found there.

In 1895, Metropolitan Hospital moved to Roosevelt Island and joined the island's City Hospital as two of the world's largest institutions. The City Hospital Building was demolished in 1994.

The Island underwent several names changes – 1921 Blackwell's to Welfare in 1972 – and from Welfare to Roosevelt. In 1969 the City of New York deeded the island to the State of New York for 99 years.

At the island's southern tip you will find the ruins of the smallpox hospital, first in our nation to receive victims of contagion and plague (1854). In 1875, America's third school of Nursing occupied much of the Island. In 1975, 8,300 apartment dwellers began joining 2,000 long term hospital residents in forming the new Roosevelt Island."

Today, Roosevelt Island has several things to recommend it – one instantly visible as you make your way across the 59th Street Bridge: *The **bright red trams** arching overhead* just to your right, making their way to the second-story station at 59th and 2nd Avenue from Roosevelt Island. Periodically, the trams are shut down for maintenance, but generally they are a reliable mode of transportation. The view from the tram is exhilarating and now and again the tram will get stuck holding the 20 or so commuters on it captive until help comes. I'm afraid of heights, so there is another slightly less fearsome way of getting to Roosevelt Island above ground and that's the small red bridge that connects from the upper third of Roosevelt

Island to *Long Island City/Astoria* (take your pick – this section of Queens is referred to by both names).

In the process of doing water color paintings I did several quick drawings from that red bridge. I'm afraid of heights. So even on the small red bridge you are 15 feet over the water and there are slats on the bridge base so you can see the river running beneath your feet. I was teetering on the slats, drawing *very quickly* so I could get off the bridge and typically, one person from Roosevelt Island tried to chat me up about where I studied art, where should she study. I tried to be nice, but my brief comments were governed by my fear of heights and the water running swiftly beneath my feet.

Roosevelt Island itself is quiet and lovely and well maintained. At the northern tip there is a small rough wild area above the lighthouse. You can pack a picnic lunch, grab a sketch book and you are set for a great afternoon of watching the boats go by – you are right by the water in the *middle of New York City*. The city has taken pains to landscape the Island so you have these inviting winding black-top roads with ever-greens either side of you luring you to explore the length of the Island, and then there is another western coastline near the launch point of the tram that has direct access to the shoreline. It's a lovely Island – probably a little too quiet for me.

One thing you see daily commuting over the bridge is bicycle traffic and lots of it – everything from people who are bonafide bike racers to messengers to the occasional out-of-shape city dweller trying to get back into shape. I tried biking back and forth to work in the last two years, but it does mean you have to have a place to park your bicycle safely and these days in New York I don't think that exists. So when I was in the bicycle shop I noticed a small aluminum scooter. The owner told me that they were the latest rage in California – and referred to it as an unstealable way to get around town (because the scooter collapses and you carry it into your office under your arm). Since I had seen even diplomats on this scooter, and since I was tired of schlepping my heavy chain on my bicycle and since the scooter was on sale, I splurged. It was after work and I had no bike gear on. I was in street clothes with a huge leather backpack thrown over my shoulder. And of course I drove my new scooter home. The kids in the neighborhood wondered how the old lady was gliding so fast down the street and ran out into the roadway to see what I was on.

I have seen the fancy motorized collapsible scooters, and their inherent speed and lack of protection in front made me think twice about buying one. But the aluminum scooter only seemed to go as fast as your right foot could push off. It wasn't as fast as running, but it was faster than walking and it seemed to reduce the weight I felt carrying my bag, so……

The next morning I put my stuff in a back pack, donned my street clothes and drove my scooter to work. I didn't like the rough ride on the sidewalk so I drove just to the right of the traffic in the street. It *was* a lot faster. I made my way south on Crescent and then onto the 59th Street Bridge. The Bridge was similarly rough riding on the scooter since the cement beneath had consistent ridges in it until you hit the blacktop span at the crest of the bridge. I was really making great time with me new toy. I got across the bridge, crossed the metal links on the other side and drove onto the rough cement roadway which descends into Manhattan. I thought, "Why should I walk…. I'll just ride my scooter a little further….." That's when I realized the scooter could go faster than I had anticipated. I knew there was a hairpin turn at the bottom of the bridge into Manhattan, and if I couldn't stop the scooter well before, I would die. One thing the bike shop owner didn't show me was how to use the brake on the scooter! I had been jumping off at the corners, figuring the scooter couldn't possible go very fast. I was in big trouble, and I knew I would have to run like hell after I jumped off the scooter to avoid serious injury.

Rather than die at the bottom of the bridge, I jumped, ran like hell (as fast as my tight skirt allowed) and hit the wall of the 59th Street Bridge (sans helmet). After landing, I realized my jaw had been displaced, so the first thing I checked was my front teeth. Both knees, both hands and my chin were bloody but I hadn't broken anything and my teeth were still in my face (a perfect five point landing!), but I was seeing stars, so I just lay on the cement propped against the wall of the bridge. A woman came by and inquired after me. I told her that I had broken my new bracelet. We found that. Then once I had my wits about me, she and I slowly walked into town. She talked to me and said she thought I was in my 20's and had expected me to jump off my scooter and do a bunch of push-ups – like the kids do. Each step I got stronger. Two blocks into town she disappeared. I know now in my heart that she was an angel. She glowed and shimmered, she helped me, and then she vanished. On the bridge you see the same people day after day. I never ever saw her again after that.

I made my way to work, called my doctor and took the train out to Whitestone. I nearly passed out several times during my commute but I get car sick in cabs, and I hate ERs. My doctor saw me, freaked out – he was pretty sure my knee was broken, stitched up chin – showed me how to use the brake on my scooter and then sent me to the ER for tests. Several x-rays and a cat scan plus the whole day shot waiting around later, I made my final interview with the ER staff. Nothing broken, but the blood from my ear indicated a head injury so I got a bunch of instructions about that. On my chart it said: "57 year old woman fell off her scooter." The discharge nurse said that the people in the hospital swore they saw me driving my scooter through the halls (something I denied) and she asked if I was going to ride the scooter again.

I left the hospital *on my scooter* and I drove it to the subway stop and then home. But it's the last time I will ever drive it. My doctor told me that he gets more kids with broken legs and arms on those scooters. I'll just keep walking.

Only infrequently do you see animals on the bridge, usually when the weather is warm. Generally they are big dogs attached to their owners by a sturdy leash. The elevated walkway is a marvelous discovery since on the traffic side you are protected by a waist-high cement barricade and on the air/water side by the natural original stone parapet with a 12 foot high mesh fence ascending into the air. When you look over the water you can imagine what it must have been like in the Middle Ages to look out over your kingdom from the watch towers of your castle. There are two magnificent stone watch towers – massive, ascending into the air 30 feet or so. There are interior rooms in those watch towers I'm sure and a delicate bronze fence protecting the roof as it slopes to meet the wall. I marvel at the workmen suspended hundreds of feet above the ground on their huge cherry-pickers as they clean that fence. As afraid of heights as I am, I love being up on the 59th Street Bridge – you feel totally protected and safe up there.

In the last year and a half the city has been updating the outer fencing on the walkway, and painting the structure itself to preserve it from the elements. The workmen are out there in all sorts of weather – and in really cold weather they think I'm totally crazy, but I'm thoroughly hooked on my morning walk into Manhattan and I have tried the Bridge after work in a pinch. It is now very well lit and the city extends grandly in every direction below, the lights glittering like jewels of every conceivable hue. At night you can really feel the energy of the city pulsing on the Bridge. That's when you can sense the soul and heartbeat of the Bridge. No matter how your day has been, the evening walk will absolutely give you an emotional lift – a natural high.

Years ago, when I first walked across the bridge, I went in the evening after work and I noticed some drug deals being made on the bridge at dusk – usually on the Manhattan side near the bottom. It made me uneasy so I only rode my bike over the bridge at night. I still see a dealer now and again, but the presence of the workmen on the Bridge has changed the entire ambiance up there. The workmen, by their mere presence, have driven the homeless that used to live on the Bridge off. There were several places that you could sleep on the Bridge without detection in absolute safety because the homeless are invisible to most people, and many homeless want to be invisible, so the 59th Street Bridge was a comfortable and inviting home for them. The homeless I saw had definite psychiatric problems and they shunned contact with people, so you and they could pass one another unmolested.

One night after my Horten class at Alvin Ailey, before my current commuting practice, I got stuck walking home at 7:30 p.m. in the dark (the subways weren't running!?!). I asked a cop who was directing traffic at the intersection on the Manhattan side of the Bridge (59th and 2nd) and he told where to get to the Bridge entrance. I ended up taking the walkway on the southern side of the 59th Street Bridge. I know the city frequently changes lane accessibility and what not so I didn't question the cop's recommendation. I was near the top of the Bridge just beginning to walk over the span, and I realized I was in the traffic lane on the *outside of the bridge* overlooking the water with about 12 inches to spare from any passing car. I was in a damned-if-you-do and damned-if-you-don't position, so I pushed on out to Queens over the bridge in the outside traffic lane – it was a real test of nerve stuffing back the panic I felt as each car pulled up behind me, honked at me, waited until I flattened myself against the inner wall and then inched past me cursing me roundly as they did. I never saw so many cars in such a tight space in my life with the full knowledge that there was a lot of black water just the other side over the edge. Just tells you that the cops don't know everything.

Depending on tonight's strike negotiations, I could begin to have lots of company on the Bridge during my commute. Not only that, I might be commuting on foot in the evening as well. It seems over the couple of years the Transit Authority has built up a huge budget surplus which large portions of, as with many publicly controlled money pots, have been diverted to some non-related areas. Case in point – a specifically large expenditure of $1.5 billion was made the day *before* the MTA contract renewal deadline. Now the transit workers want a cut. Who could blame them?

But part of what they are threatening to strike about is increased subsidy to medical insurance, since at the moment they have had to begin to pay a portion of their medical premiums out of pocket. They also want an 8% raise – don't we all? And they also want life-time pension after retirement with retirement as early as age 55. A beginning motorman earns $42,000 per year – overtime included in that amount. They have to be a high school graduate. Many of the new hires get a higher-paying initial job with the Transit Authority because they know someone in the union.

Compare that to the standard secretarial salary (these days without experience - $30,000 a year) – and mind you the employer wants a college graduate, someone who types well and preferably knows short-hand and looks nice. She will also have to pay a portion of her insurance premium. There will be no pension in her future – if she's lucky she will have a 401K after she is vested – if she lasts five years. She will have to invest in good clothes and put up with a lot of one-on-one in-your-face pressure. And she will have to pay roughly $1,500 for a one room apartment in Queens or Brooklyn – Manhattan is much more expensive. And the MTA wants to strike. I think all the secretaries in New York should strike – the city would stop dead!

I have frequently been hijacked by the subway out in Queens. Under the guise of construction – the trains won't run, or will only partially run – or you have to connect to a bus. On one such Saturday afternoon there actually was a crew on the tracks. I counted 43 workers – of the 43 workers, 2 were working. The rest of them were either standing around, eating or drinking something – but certainly not working. I have been told by relatives of transit workers that the supervisor of any given crew will only work several members of his crew while the remainder of the crew sits. They maintain this prerogative so they are covered if they ever really need all of them. Show me any secretary who has that kind of arrangement with her boss, and my suspicion is that she is doing more than typing.

Yes they may complain that their hours are long, the work grubby and passenger attitudes are bad, but I also know PhDs who are pumping gas earning much less without any benefits living hand-to-mouth. And then these yahoos wait until just before Christmas to jerk the city around. Bah – humbug!

I'm at the tail end of a rough week. My former pianist wants to conduct, so he is becoming the willing slave to a less-than-top opera conductor in New York. He is a very deft if glib musician and he certainly gets the job done efficiently. As a result I decided to go back to a previous pianist – a really fine musician, crack reader and big player. However, he is manic-depressive and became very unreliable which is why we parted company years back.

I decided to have a rehearsal Sunday night with him before Christmas to gauge how it would probably work. He gave me the creeps and I withdrew as gracefully as common decency allowed. I believe we all silently think "There but for the grace of God go I" when we see the homeless on the street – many of whom were dumped there in the 1970's when NYC decided to save money and empty its asylums. I have a case of the guilts walking away from my former pianist, but I have to walk away. I fear for his future, and the entire feel of our rehearsal still lingers and will serve as a constant reminder to me that you simply have to truck on, stay healthy, alert, aggressive and able or you can end up on the streets here. That's one thing New York City has – the very best and the very worst – the very talented who frequently starve in their dedication – and the superficial glib talents who glad-hand their way to the right connections and earn a fortune. That's the not-so-pretty underbelly of the city. New York is unforgiving of anyone who is old, infirm and poor – they have it the worst – the working poor - and the city runs on their backs.

This morning, it was raining lightly and it's the day we exchange holiday gifts at work, so I was loaded down with packages and could use a rolling cart to schlepp with. It was still a very pleasant walk. Particularly just over the crest of the span as you look downward toward the Manhattan side. The drizzle actually reminded me of winter in London – a certain very grey yet warm embrace of the weather.

It reminded me of an inexpensive pension in London. The pension was roughly 3 miles from Covent Garden where I was going to audition. If you have seen *As Time Goes By* on TV – the streets look like that. Only the row of houses were older, less imposing and more thinly constructed. The main office of the pension was just beneath the stairwell toward the back. The stairway was open with white scrolling and a very ancient red/green/yellow floral wool carpeting ran the entire length of the stairway right out to the front foyer. I stayed in a very modest second story room that had a creaky twin bed with an old chenille bedspread on it. The bedroom reminded me of a 1940's kitchen – the cabinetry that sort of enameled off-white but chipped finish with an ersatz green marble top. The entire set of drawers wobbled badly if you tried to open anything, so I placed my suitcase on the available folding chair and made do.

Not only was the room on the shabby yet homey side, but the window faced out to the street and at night a fluorescent sign flashed on and off pinkly illuminating the room through the old lace curtains. One feature I had not bargained for was the leaky windows. January in London is warmer than Wisconsin in the same month, but in Wisconsin people freeze so everything is very well insulated. Not so this little room. Who would think that the inviting warm fog of the day could chill you straight to the bone at night? I did not get a lot a sleep. I was too cold.

There was one bathroom for the entire house with a big tub and a very strange operating commode. You had to know the "sweet spot" to make it flush properly. I wasted much effort trying to get it to work properly while realizing that if it didn't work, everyone would think that I was a very untidy American.

Actually, I ended up staying at the Pension twice – once for my ENO audition and second time for my Covent Garden audition. One thing the Pension had was an enormous and varied breakfast.

I Intend to Become a Professional Opera Singer

I grew up on a farm in the middle of Wisconsin, and attended a parochial school grades 1 through 8 and survived the rather straight conservative religious constraints that defined the school's hierarchy. Looking back, I was too dumb to be independent. That came later. And that school defined discrimination. The Missouri Synod Lutheran church had the protestant control of the little town of Merrill, Wisconsin (10,000 population). The townspeople away from the parochial rigidity were quite accepting and tolerant, and the high school there was really very good.

My first church solo was at the age of 9 in front of an entire congregation (about 500 people) standing in the front of the church. It was easy. It was fun. I could tell they liked my voice and I had no concept of nerves. The organist was 200 feet overhead and played with his back to me. I was hooked.

I had a voice teacher very briefly who couldn't sing and didn't know how to place the voice. Since I was musical I lead the alto section in the choir because I read music - my very first big blunder. It set my path for my entire singing career until I corrected it many years later. I was actually a coloratura soprano with a range to B flat above high C.

In time the tax base changed once I was in high school. My freshman year was in Merrill and a really wonderful high school with broadminded generous teachers throughout. I was awarded a scholarship to Stephens Point for two weeks to a music clinic, and by sheer dumb luck I was taught by a lyric tenor, Thomas Fitzsimmons (Juilliard trained) who had sung in Europe. In less than two weeks he corrected the lineup of the voice and he confirmed that I was a coloratura soprano. I easily sang the high F over and over again. Because I was the youngest child in the family, I got attention by throwing my speaking voice down (another huge mistake). Because of the taxing districts I was transferred to Wausau High.

Wausau High was hide bound on receiving honors and referring to their honors. They felt it was better to isolate classes by IQ (a very bad idea), so I was stuck with the high IQs and after arriving at Wausau High I was awarded the lead soprano role in the operetta presented later that year. Because of that attention, several of the guys in my honors English class decided to bully me. I don't intend to make this story about the bullying, but suffice it to say, I was suicidal by my junior year. I read the entire psychiatric section in the library to try to help myself. I tolerated the bullying until one of our neighbors shot our shepherd mix dog IN OUR FIELD. The maniac shot over the heads of two children sitting on a big boulder directly in his line of fire. I was so upset by this that the next morning I was near tears on the bus (the bullying began there and they stopped when they saw the tears). At school two of the worst culprits started in on me in the hallway, and I turned to both of them saying, "Roger, LEAVE ME ALONE!??!!" Everett was standing behind him grinning. The smile dropped from his face when I began to beat the crap out of Roger with my fists, and I did not stop. It was in the hallway and no one was around. I remember I was wearing a newly made shirtwaist dress in a gorgeous shade of green. I didn't even damage my dress. The years of loading haybales on a moving wagon gave me superb balance and a dead-eye accuracy contact with Roger's gut.

That year our choir director broker her hip, and since I was their pianist, I took over the class to keep it going. After a week the principal came to observe and he said, "I'm going to let you do it. It works." We had another replacement teacher who got sick but I handled the choir and girls glee club and taught a few voice students on the side for the upcoming Spring state competitions.

Because I had been exposed to Thomas Fitzsimmons at Stevens Point, that's where I went to the UW Stevens Point as a freshman, I assumed that he would be my voice teacher.. Alas Thomas Fitzsimmons wasn't there. There was a tenor with a good sound but who forced, a baritone who sang without any real support and a soprano who sounded like homogenized milk. I ended up with the baritone and sang the role of Frasquita in Carmen (as secondary coloratura role). After a year of the baritone who had real strange ideas about vocal classifications and the appropriate age to begin singing big repertoire, my voice was in tatters again. I was lucky enough to land in piano lessons for my proficiency with an egghead from Eastman School of Music. After he broke my inhibitions down, I thrived with him. But my voice was a huge mess and I was very unhappy.

My sister had gone from pre-med at the Wausau Extension to a piano major at the UW Madison and she had told me wonderful stories about this beautiful coloratura soprano who taught at the UW Madison. I will call her Bethany Peterson. This is where the real Sue Hassel finds her identity. And of all the people I was exposed to she had the greatest impact on me as an artist, musician and singer. I was eager to leave UW Stephens Point since my voice was in pieces, so at the earliest opportunity I jumped ship and entered the UW Madison on probation. It was some 20 years later that the Stevens Point college became part of the fully vested University of Wisconsin. Hence my probationary status.

I will never forget the first week in Madison. It was a real University town with so many strange nationalities in attendance. I saw flowing saris and Pakistani trousers on women. It was all very heady and exciting and new. The registration week was a horror. The campus was sprawled over a few miles with Lake Mendota bordering it. Bascom Hill was a visible impressive landmark with the administration building at the top and the Music School at its base. The Music School was an older building erected in the 1920s or so, complete with clock tower and beautiful performance hall that seated about 600. The acoustics were stunning in that space. Lathrop Hall was the next large building just up the hill on the left. That was where modern dance and ballet as in "dance majors" was taught. When I arrived the dance major program was placed under the school of physical education. However as time went by UW Madison acquired some very ferocious credentials in modern dance and ballet and offered it as a fine arts major..

Registration was a once a semester nightmare. I went to the Armory on Langdon Street that had the biggest floor space with a fenced off upper level that runners normally used. However on registration day that upper level had people spread all along it with their boxes of computer punchcard class listings. There were large sections labeled by letters A to Z delineating Fine Arts, Education, Agricultural Studies, Humanities, Physical Education, Graduate School, Undergraduate Music, Undergraduate Liberal Arts etc. .on and on it went. Each registrant was given a coded list that ran two pages. You looked up your major, and then followed the impromptu directions posted all over the place. You had been provided a syllabus of course requirements for your major, and when it was private music teaching the contact number and location on campus of your advisor. It took me two days to fight through it all. The large classes that had 30-40 students per class went fast. There were always multiple sections available and then you simply signed, asked further questions of the people at the desks and you were registered. However, the B.M. and M.M. in Music was a different kettle of fish. I was readily placed in chorus, music theory, music appreciation, early music, and class voice or class piano if you were a rank beginner. I signed up for modern dance instead of gym so that was done. However at 3 pm I left the Armory and trudged on up Bascom Hill to the music school. There were 5 people ahead of me. The first one was arguing with the acceptability of his proposed thesis. He was a graduate student, as I recall anthropology. However, he wanted to study piano privately on the side. The advisor explained to him that until all students had been assigned to the teacher he was asking about for that semester, he just had to wait. If there was a vacancy after all the music majors had been assigned, he would need a special confirmation from his major professor that he had the time to study piano and work on his thesis. I groaned, waited awhile, asked the next guy ahead of me to hold my place and ran for the john.

When I came back there was just one person ahead of me. Apparently the others had an easy confirmation since they had been at the University the previous semester. I was lucky. I requested to study with Bethany Petersen. The advisor was not sure that I had enough background to work with her since she only worked with the best singers. I begged and pleaded and explained that I had grown up on farm and played piano some; that I had been at Stephens Point and had sung the role of Frasquita in Carmen and that I danced publicly in the opera with a brief modern dance background. His face softened. "Sit outside please for a minute." I left and he closed the door. He made a phone call and hung up. The door opened. He had called Bethany and she seemed interested in my background, so she accepted me in the voice major program. He told me I had better work hard. Then he asked me about my level of piano. I explained that I had four years privately, that I had taken over the choruses and glee clubs in high school when the teacher broke her hip and had managed that for five months. He made another call. This time I could hear his side. "She doesn't have a big piano background, but she took over the choruses when her instructor broke her hip." His final words, "Now? Okay I will send her right over."

"I'm not sure you should be in class piano, so go to the third floor and check in with the secretary. Two of the piano teachers are still there. They want to hear you." I responded, "I didn't bring my music," and he wished me luck.

I sat outside with the secretary, and heard some incredible Beethoven being played, and I really began to panic. I never played by ear. I memorized or read score cold on sight. Finally the playing stopped. Then they talked for a few minutes. The door swung open and a very tall, very bald man with laughing blue eyes wearing a rumpled white shirt rolled up to the elbows greeted me. His associate was a dignified grey haired man with horn rimmed glasses, clothed in a light blue shirt and LL Bean trousers. I was immediately put off by the bald headed man and intimidated. They pointed to the piano, and so I sat down. "What do you have to play for us?" And I responded, "I just came from the Armory and was referred here by an advisor. I'm a voice major, and I will be studying with Bethany Petersen. The advisor sent me here. I don't have anything memorized right now. Do you have anything that I can sight read?" They looked at each other, and the bald one said, "How about some Mozart?" "Do you have any Brahms?" "Let's hear Mozart first." I kept my fingers crossed that I had seen it on Beverly's piano someplace. Whenever Beverly was out with friends and I had the house to myself, I read through all her music. No such luck but the first movement wasn't difficult, and then I played into the slow movement the first time through and was interrupted, "Okay, not bad. How about the Opus 118 G minor Ballade?" That I loved. That I had played. I sailed through it, and thought I was off the hook. Not really. Then they threw me into a Haydn sonata. It looked like an easy read. I was so freaked I played it in E flat major and got through it. Then the one with the glasses said, "Wrong key. Check the key signature." I played it again, this time in E major. One final curve ball. They gave me a page of orchestral open score to read. I thought, "Will this ever end, it looks awful, but - I got away with it, - JUST!"

I left the room and the secretary told me to wait. More talking behind the door. The secretary was called in. She came back out, sat down at her desk and called my advisor. "Yes, no class piano for her. Saul is going to take a chance on her. If necessary let's see about a piano minor."

The secretary turned to me, "Your advisor is tired. It's been a long day. Report to him tomorrow at 9 a.m." "I should be going to my first class." "Don't worry about it, you can miss the first class. It will be chaotic at best." I murmured my thanks, and left.

I had no idea that registration could be so complicated – particularly with private teachers. I made the assumption that any new students were the proverbial blank slates that important teachers left their individual stamp on, and that was that. That those teachers, not having any background on an individual student worked with the next student coming through the door. I met with my advisor as directed, and then he asked a lot of questions regarding my background. And he filled out a large form based on what I was saying in response to his questions. Then I had four difference smaller cards that had to be filled in which were entered into the Music School database. My advisor explained to me that I had been very lucky. First of all Bethany Petersen accepted me. It is likely that had I not taken over the choruses in high school or sung Frasquita in Carmen I would have been passed on to a newly assigned but very qualified junior-standing voice teacher. I could infer from the way the advisor spoke that Bethany had a huge reputation and wide ranging influence in musical circles in Wisconsin and Madison. I also found out that Saul Carlton enjoyed a new kid-on-the-block reputation that signaled to me I would be hanging on for dear life with a wild-man who wrote his own rules, and had a huge solo piano reputation. It was unheard of that someone with such a modest backround as I had even got past the front door. The advisor wished me luck, shook my hand and directed me back to the secretary in the piano department. The secretary had her calls forwarded to another person, and then took me to a small room off to the side of the main office. "Ms. Hassel, you have been very fortunate. Bethany Petersen is accepting you on probation because you have sung a leading role in an opera. She is also impressed that you took over the choruses in high school. She is interested in your piano and modern dance background." I thought to myself, "Frasquita is a pivotal role, but it is a secondary role. - Modern dance?!" The secretary went on, "Saul Carlton is interested that you taught the choruses in high school and played piano to be able to accomplish that. He was also taken with your ability to correct misreading the Haydn the first time and then playing it the second time in the correct key. Both versions worked – but making the quick fingering adjustment so smoothly was noticed. Saul Carlton has been with us for two years now and in that time he has played several solo recitals both in Madison and run-outs to other locations as well as a concerto with orchestra, and has drawn some really fine pianists to our school. So you have some incredible people to study with. Make good use of it." I was elated, and then sudden dread took over..

"Now, you need to buy music immediately. For voice, purchase the first main book of Schubert songs in the high key Peters edition; Alte Meister des Bel Cantos both volumes, high key Peters edition, The first three volumes of the National edition of Handel's Soprano arias, and the Mozart Song collection in the high key. There is only one volume and Dover publishes it. For piano buy Bach Well tempered Clarvier both volumes Peters Edition, Beethoven Sonatas – two volumes Henle Edition. The Brahms piano works Volume 2, and the Hanon exercises, both volumes." "Where do I buy the music?" "There is a store up on State Street to buy all of this. They know your teachers, and they make sure they have it all in stock. If they don't have everything right away, they will order it for you immediately. Your first lesson with Bethany will be Friday morning at 8:00 a.m. And your first lesson with Saul will be the following Monday at 4 p.m. in the afternoon. He's out of town for the remainder of this week".

I had to run back to the Union to telephone my sister, Beverly: "Help. You are not going to believe the amount of music I have to buy. Where am I going to get the money?" "The piano music is expensive. The vocal will not be a big deal. They are modest volumes. However you can substitute Schirmer for the Bach and for the Beethoven. After all, you are looking at a piano minor. Schirmer will be accurate, the print will be bigger, and half the time no one reads the notations in the Henle scores. Just explain that's all you can afford. I will lend you the money to begin with."

My sister had been teaching piano in a modest university setting in Appleton and had just been hired to the Oshkosh branch of the University of Wisconsin as Professor of Piano. That night we had a long phone call. "Well, you are working with the best pianist at the school right now. That's a good sign. And Bethany is a beautiful singer, but I have heard some stories. She can be difficult. I have seen her reduce pianists to tears."

On my way out the door from the Music School I saw an ad for a library assistant. I wrote the info down and later that day I called the Music Library. I met with the head librarian. He was meticulously neat, distant, precise and didn't miss anything, and I got the job. I started the following week. He took pity on me for the first week of classes.

One week for me to get used to the University. Thank heaven for my bicycle. My dorm, was on the other end of campus past Liz Waters on the other side of Bascom Hill. That afternoon I had my first advanced honors English class. The advisor was right. The entire class was getting to know the teacher, her background, the class order of reading materials that we would be tested on and last but not least a gargantuan term paper assignment.

An hour after that, I entered Lathrop Hall and looked for my modern dance class on the bulletin board. Lathrop Hall was a very old, very creaky building, clearly designed for dance and gymnastics – 6 stories high, each story had three large rehearsal studios with mirror flanked walls and wooden floors that had the highest gloss I have seen on any floor. My first class was with Joe Templeton, a gorgeous man with light red hair tightly shaved to the head, huge blue eyes, a dancer's tight body and a fiery intense attitude. Our class was 50 people strong, men and women all clad in black leotards and barefoot. We started with some simple warmups – accompanied by a guy sitting near the door playing on two big drums with his bare hands. We had to function entirely in the center with no barre to hang on to for balance. At Stevens Point I had been exposed to the Duncan method. This was quite different. Clearly the majority of my class members had ballet backgrounds. After 45 minutes there was a break. By that time I had sized up the best dancer in the class and when we resumed class I carefully placed myself within diagonal eyeshot of her for the remainder of the class. It was the first day of class and no one bothered me. Everyone was trying to survive the class without any major gaffes. The second 45 minutes went a lot better, since once we stood at the sides of the hall, the drummer went to the piano and played as the teacher demonstrated a complicated sequence including a pirouette and two tour jetes running the diagonal of the room. When it came my turn, I nailed the entire sequence, since by then I had seen at least 3 or 4 rather good dancers do it before me. Great class, and quite different from Duncan. For me Duncan is an acquired taste since the turns and hip placement are more passively executed, with more back and forth movement of the shoulders and torso generally. I found out later that this was a Graham class. It was a good thing. It felt more logical in the body. After class I talked to that really good dancer and asked how long she had been dancing etc. She began in ballet at age 5 in Paris, and came to modern very late. I asked her if they taught ballet at Lathrop. She confirmed that, but warned me that I would begin with very young people around me since the University had an early start program for the majors, many of whom never had ballet. After class I went to the office at Lathrop and asked about the beginning ballet class, and received a quizzical look since I was rather old to be in a beginning ballet class. I asked the secretary if I could take beginning ballet for Phys Ed credit. I could, and I found another class that ran the same time Monday and Wednesday and yes it would qualify for the Phys Ed credit. They changed my records and on Wednesday I would show up at ballet. I was told I would need some soft ballet slippers, as well as the location of another shop in town where they sold them at a student discount. It was close by so right after class I ran to the store and bought a pair of ballet slippers. The store was a wonderland of beautiful leotards, skirts, tights and tutus. I spoke with the owner and she said, "We have a section for the new dance majors at Lathrop. Do you have a black leotard, black tights?" I nodded my head in ascent.

"Good. Let's see if we have soft ballet slippers in your size." She pulled out a carton of exquisitely soft leather pink shoes with recessed soles and modest elastic bands, - far more beautiful and supple than anything I had ever worn. And I learned that you wore them roughly a half size smaller than any street shoe. I walked around in them – no cushion whatsoever, but an incredible suppleness rising up to demi-pointe and arching the foot. Clearly the only place you wore these special shoes was on a dance prepared floor that was smooth and even on landing and slightly raised (roughly 4" of space between the surface we landed on and the base floor beneath that had designed partitions to raise the floor one danced on). I asked to see a pair of pointe shoes out of curiosity, and she pulled a pair out. That was quite a different shoe that demanded a complete physical mechanical adjustment to be able to dance on, leap on and land on. I thought very quickly, "I will never be that good." I thanked the store owner for showing me the shoes and more importantly her willingness to give me a vague idea of what ballet dancing was about.

I headed back to the dorm. I had missed dinner, but was told there were some leftovers if I ran fast. I ran to my room, dropped my books, shoes and music on the bed, slammed the door, locked it and ran back to the lunch hall. The food was cold, but it was good, and tasted delicious. Perhaps not as good as ACE food in Stephens Point or as highly caloric, but probably better for me.

After my supper, I took a shower, towel dried my hair, jumped into my PJs and threw a robe on. I was third in line to the shared phone at the end of the hall. I sat on the floor and waited my turn.

I pulled out my phone card and called Beverly. She picked up first, "Well, tell me about your day." She was pleased that I was able to get cheaper copies of the music. The Beethoven Henley editions were out of stock for two weeks, so I substituted Schirmer. "You may have just lucked out. You can't wait two weeks before you show up with music, so they can't fault you for that. Do you have the receipt?" "Yep, all of them." "Well then, you might skin by on the Schirmer editions. He will fuss some, but you are a voice major, and aside from the index of reference comments in the Henley, there is virtually no difference and the copy is really clean and big." "I was able to get all of the demanded editions for the vocal music, all of it. So I won't start behind the eight ball. Where do I practice? If I have to show up and sing well on Friday at 8 a.m. for Bethany I would like to check out the scores and read through them, and practicing with a pitch pipe in the middle of a vacant lot won't cut it." "There are annexes all over the place, but Bethany has her studio at 508 State Street. Go there and sign up for a practice room on the top floor. She's on the main floor near the small hall. That way she won't hear you before Friday. You can get the drop on her."

"Sounds like you really like the dance classes. They will be a good stress buster. And honors English, How did that happen?" "I have no idea. Tomorrow morning at 8 am I start theory, then wait for an hour, then music appreciation later. After that I should be able to sneak up to 508 State Street. Is there a formal signup sheet before the fact? Do I call in or what?" "Depends if anyone is there to answer. There are other annexes further out south of the university. If you are really stuck, you will find something there. It's a walk out there but you have your bicycle. You have privacy and usually you get a space to work in on the fly. Also, the walls will not have ears at that location." "The walls have ears?" "Yes, there is no expectation of privacy anywhere. Bethany frequently has her spies out and they report back. That's just a heads up from me." "I will ask the music office the location of the southern annexes. I prefer that. I don't like spies."

I organized my shelves with the stuff from my suitcase. I shared a closet with my roommate. She had really nice clothes, much more fashion conscious than I. I still hadn't met her. It seemed the music school was spread out all over, but the music school was in the old section of the University. That night at 10 pm my room mate arrived. She was black and she was from Milwaukee. She was studying for an education degree. After hearing her friends talking, I realized that her background was worlds apart from mine. She had lived in Milwaukee all her life and was used to running down to Chicago on the weekend. She had a compact car so she was far more mobile than I was, and apparently fearless.

The thought of the Chicago traffic on the skyline – I drove it once with Beverly on board for an audition. The time was so tight that I practiced in the car as I drove. Five car lanes making the loop around the city packed with cars driving FAST, and no chance for error. Drivers as they passed me were wondering what I was doing. Beverly saw the drivers passing us trying to understand what I was doing at the wheel. She vacilated between laughing hysterically and yelling periodically, "You cut him off." Lynette, my roommate had to be insane to make that drive to see friends on the weekend. Give me the privacy of open fields where I can practice, live animals that are fun to watch and the clean air out in the country.

The week seemed to drag, vacillating between busy and preoccupied with dread and excitement, even though I was able to pick through the vocal albums and two Beethoven sonatas. I never had to sight read vocally. That thought terrified me. Sometimes I would try and depending upon the composer I either sailed through without a hitch or crashed immediately and ended up carefully picking through my vocal line with some accompaniment beneath phrase by phrase. I found that going slower I could make the various vowel/consonant accommodations with the general placement of the sound in my mouth or further back when higher easily. Faster, and I had trouble getting my tongue out of the way to do the job. I figured one Handel aria, two Mozart songs and two Schubert songs. I would see if I could somehow direct the conversation after working with Bethany.

Friday arrived, I biked from the dorm onto the campus turning east on State Street. Very few people out there at 7:30 a.m., traffic was light and I made my way up State Street toward the capital stopping at the address 508 State Street. Not much to set the building apart from the neighboring shops and restaurants, although I noticed a bar just West of 508 State Street. The front door was open and as I climbed the stairs, I heard complete silence. Apparently not many musicians hauled out at this hour. At the top of the stairs I noticed a small hall to the right containing a small stage at the other end. I was close to Bethany's office. I sat down on a chair and waited. Ten minutes later I heard the front door open below and steady footsteps echoing in the hallway. As Bethany arrived at the top steps I noticed the lightweight beige suede hat on her head, the silk scarf around her neck and the well-made L.L. Bean khaki jacket. I was too busy taking in her face to notice much else. She was older than I had expected, handsome and occupied the immediate space she entered completely. I jumped to my feet throwing my backpack over my shoulder automatically and followed her to the first office on the right. I could tell she was sizing me up in my jeans and windbreaker. "Did you walk here?" "My bicycle is parked outside." I observed her face reacting to my informal dress, and then relaxing when I mentioned my bicycle. "Which dorm are you living at?" When I confirmed the location, she responded, "You need a bicycle from that location. It's pretty far out." I surmised that she had arrived by cab. Her shoes were too elegant to have walked any great distance. She took her coat, hat and scarf off and hung them in a small closet near the door. She turned to me and explained that that there was a mandatory weekly Master Class that she held in the auditorium on site from from 6 pm to 8 pm on Wednesdays in which her students could share their music-making progress. I look startled and she clarified that she planned the programs for each master class and there would be no last minute surprises. The more-advanced students would begin each session so new students could learn from the older ones, and that over the period of a year all of her students would perform. Anyone invited to the classes was encouraged to contribute their observations, thoughts and comments. I surmised from her tone of voice that the entire class had to be a positive experience for performers and attendees alike. I made a mental note that I had my first piano lesson with Saul Carlton on Monday at 4:00 p.m.so I had no conflict.

I dropped my backpack and jacket on the floor next the closet door and stood aside until she sat behind the piano.. She was a very handsome woman, mid 60's with incredible wavy grey hair cut close to the neckline in the back and arching gracefully from a widows peak in front framing a beautiful oval face with the most intense dark eyes that took my measure in less than a minute. I returned the gaze steadily until she broke it as she talked. She was dressed in the most exquisitely-cut loden green suit with a floral silk blouse beneath, tied at the neck in a loose graceful bow. I was perhaps 3" taller than Bethany. She wore expensive black walking shoes to complete the ensemble. She shook my hand, and I found the grip feminine with a perfectly smooth supple hand and graceful fingers. She wore flesh colored nail enamel. My callused farm girl hand dwarfed her grip. I have never felt skin that soft until many years later before my grandmother died. Our handshake was ambiguous. I could not size her up by her grip, so I steadily watched her eyes for any clue behind the impeccable façade. I likely came off as a country bumpkin. I emulated my father who was common spoken and approachable, and we both faced everyone with the same middle American directness. It allowed the observer to quickly assess the stranger as friend or foe immediately. Any diversion of the eyes or foot shuffle telegraphed an unsteady ambivalence in any ensuing communication. I read in my first impression of Bethany a cultivated finesse and refinement, and a difficult earlier life.

We began to vocalize. I asked if we could begin in the second octave, and explained that I had no low notes to start. The top always worked but the area from middle C to the fifth above was tenuous to start, or if not tenuous, then the muscles in my throat grabbed. We began and she quickly realized that the first octave was very unstable. The top of the voice just worked without any thought. The bottom, that was something else. She gave me a five tone scale from the top to the lower fifth in the first octave. Then we worked the same notes with different vowel combinations. And finally there was a level of stability alternating vowels for the passage EEH, AY, AH and OH. Finally after a rough start the first octave began to sound accurately. The top was simply placed and always worked. She asked me about my background, and I explained that I got stuck in the alto section of the church choir because I read music. Finally, she had a very clear picture of how to proceed. We went over some random phrases with words (even in translation to English, the content of what you are singing will change the sound because that is how your brain collectively processes the image of the words and music and the throat reacts spontaneously). A few more minutes, still not satisfied, Bethany placed me away from the piano in the middle of the room and told me to bend over at the waist allowing my arms to hang loosely at the side. Then I was told to sing on one pitch eeh, ay, ah, oh, ooh connected in one phrase, and immediately like magic the throat was free, nothing grabbed, and the sound of the middle E a third above middle C quietly filled the space. By the end of the session I had been able to successfully vocalize 2 octaves plus a third at the top, and at the end of the lesson the bottom notes worked. She asked about my speaking voice, and I said my entire family had high singing voices and terrible rough low speaking voices. When you work outside on the fields and have to communicate with one another, you yell. When you have to call for the cows, you yell. But I could infer by the direction of the questions that she disapproved of the yelling and the rough speaking voice. But she approved of the physical athleticism and asked if I ever had a dance course. I told her about the Duncan classes, and that I was enrolled at Lathrop in beginning ballet rather than phys ed. She thought that was a good idea. Finally we attempted to read Mozart's Abendemfindung. She played very well, and I got through it without a hitch. That was my favorite Mozart song and I owned the record with Elizabeth Schwarzkopf singing and Gerald Moore accompanying. There is one very elegant turn on the last grupetto of the penultimate phrase that must be eloquently placed so that the cadencing phrase becomes the quiet satisfying resolution to the entire piece. If you are nervous the support won't be steady and it quivers precisely at the point of resolution on the English words "as the finest pearl is." It begins on the top line F just where the mid voice begins to shift back and up a little. If you can think the sound really heady and begin the phrase as soft as you imagine it should be, it works. However, if you have never sung that part of the range quietly free of tension and anticipation of the fifth above that sound "die schoenste Perle sein" the first pitch will be too loud and the singer immediately pulls back the volume to finish the phrase, but that quick volume adjustment nearly destroys the phrase. I got hung up. Bethany pointed to her mid-section and began pulsating the upper belly just below the belt. That suppleness applied precisely the amount of support that rendered the desired emotional resolution to the phrase. When I sang it, it was accurate but athletic sounding. When Bethany sang it, it was the most lovely sound I ever heard. It was the sound that quietly filled the space and it had the quiet shimmer of a pearl. That sound, even at this writing, is embedded in my memory. It was so right, so apt and so lovely.

And then like a too brief lovely dream, the lesson ended. Bethany went to a file cabinet and pulled out an old handwritten manuscript book of vocalizes and gave it to me to work on as well as two Handel arias. I felt as though I had been transported to some fine house in Vienna where everything was formal and gentile. I was the mouse in the corner taking it all in.

I drove back to the music building, parked my bicycle in the back, entered the first floor, checked the bulletin board and walk downstairs into the basement to the next class, Music Theory. The sun had finally come out bathing the dreary classroom in bright light from the two windows to the south, the age of the room obvious by the bare chipped radiators along the wall, the walls covered with two different colors of paint that met at one end. Twenty of us were in the class, and the professor, Mr. Hetfeld, was running late. Suddenly the door swung open and in walked a handsome man of average size (reminded me of Ernest Hemingway) holding a box of flowers with one hand while balancing a briefcase with the other. He took in the class with one glance and began, "My daughter just joined a commune and became a hippy, a flower child, and so I thought I would bring flowers to class to share with you. Please take one." He made his way around the class stopping in front of each student grinning as we each tentatively took a long stemmed perennial. I sensed that he was having us on, judging from the twinkle in his eye. Some of the attendees chuckled self-consciously, others watched quietly as I did. After most of the flowers were gone, and about a third of them remained in the box, which he closed, he left the room briefly and returned minus the box, saying, "I just walked into another class and left the rest of the flowers with them. They're still scratching their heads." At that comment the class laughed collectively. He pulled a sheaf of papers from his briefcase and passed the batch out to our class, each student helping himself and then passing the batch on. This time no extras.

Perhaps the flowers and the back story were to indicate to us how "hip" he was (after all this was before many of the demonstrations in Wisconsin and we were just hearing about the Manson killings and talk of communes in California). He abruptly changed course on to the syllabus for the class that he had just given us. Simple, straightforward 2-1/2 pages. However as simple as it looked, judging from the way his head worked, this class could be a pip, merely interesting or unreliable and quirky. Typically any first day of any class, you receive materials, and if things are straightforward the materials are just for reference. The teacher had a way of lingering on certain things, and I surmised that he was more of a composer than a teacher. That was his passion. By the end of class I had a good set of notes to begin with and reserved my judgment for some later date.

I asked class members where people ate lunch, and was told that there was a Rennabaum's drug store that sold sandwiches or Lorenzo's, an Italian restaurant at the end of the block across the street or the student Union near the water – that was more expensive generally. So I trudged over to Rennies, bought a sandwich and returned to Bascom Hill where other students were sitting outside on the lawn and enjoyed the sunny day. I was glad I had my jacket on though.

I decided to check with the music office and ask about the locations of the various rehearsal annexes. It took some time. In some cases the annexes did not have an onsite supervisor, which meant you had to check with the music office by phone. You could get stuck on hold. I asked if it was fair game to just show up and see if a room was open. The secretary said that would work, but there would be a sign-up sheet near the front door, which was kept reasonably up-to-date. If there was no one signed into the room, and there were others still available, then to feel free to sign in and take the room for the time you needed (posting all of this on the sign in sheet at the front door). I groaned, but then I thought, try it and see.

I jumped on my bike and made my way south two blocks and then beneath an underpass – two blocks later and I turned left and found a building labeled UW Music Annex. I parked my bike on the outside stands and went in. In 15 minutes the next slot would open and I was lucky since it appeared there were at least five rooms open. I helped myself. The floors creaked as I ascended the stairs to the third floor where several rooms were adjacently open.

I opened a window and looked out and saw easily two blocks of wide-open overgrown space. The day was crisp and clear and I began vocalizing. Then I took Bethany's hand-written vocalize book out and spent 30 minutes acquainting myself with the way she worked. Finally I started singing the Handel arias as I played piano, and read through 3/4s of the Alte Meister des Bel Canto Book 1 – found many beautiful things in the first volume. The second volume covered more ensemble things, many things written for male voices – a few good things for high soprano. Finally I opened the main Schubert album – another real treat to read through – one fabulous tune after the other, some challenging piano accompaniments. I began with the Schoene Muellerin – the tessitura generally was higher in that cycle. Although by the end of the hour I had made my way to the back of the book, and there were many songs that lay generally very well for my voice. I finished the session reading through my Schirmer soprano aria collection and a related coloratura soprano aria collection that I had acquired while at Stephens Point (the two bootleg scores that I brought with me from home). When I ran into a problem, I used one of Bethany's vocalizes to work through the section on combined vowel variations. As

I worked, generally the top of the voice was naturally placed, so I would begin at the end of the aria and work back to the beginning w Stephany's notes. It had never occurred to me to alternate several vowels one after the other on the same breath stream in the same phrase. As long as I didn't try to sing real words in the first octave, I was okay and the voice worked smoothly. The minute I began using consonants, things fell apart. I would have to ask Bethany about that. I had three favorite arias that I retreated to that I had been singing for a year. Dinorah's Shadow Song, Marguerite's Jewel Song and the Act IV Trovatore Scene. As long as I could retreat into straight coloratura figurations, everything worked. When I had to deal with the Roi de Thule section of the Marguerite it was less good. The tongue pulled and the resonance placement was hit or miss. So I went back to the five vowel rotation vocalize throughout the problem areas and it corrected things. Once back to the words, I was at sea.

I had not taken any time to work through my piano music since I had begun to make real progress vocally. So I placed my written request on the wall chart in the foyer for Monday morning at 8 a.m.to 11:00 a.m.in the same room. The piano was a serviceable Chickering with a solid action. Before dealing with Saul at 4 p.m. on Monday I had two hours to cram and get myself settled and in the process unload my dread for awhile at least. I would return on Sunday afternoon for three hours to work the voice and piano the day before.

Moderately pleased with myself I left the annex and returned to Lathrop Hall for my first ballet class. I wasn't the oldest person in the class. We had four really young girls (pre-dance majors), three or four exquisitely proportioned adult dancers, two guys and me. I clearly had the biggest bust and shoulders of all of them. I rounded my shoulders forward in embarrassment. I was the biggest person in the class (that includes the instructor and the men!?!). The teacher explained the turn out, and where it began with the rolled back shoulders and an arched back which made the head lift out high above the shoulders on a lengthened neck – similar to a flower at the top of an elegant stem – with the legs turning out from the hip in one clean line – stomach pulled up and in. We hung on to the barre with the left hand, arched our backs and lifting our heads erectly, extended our free arm straight out to the right and then overhead with our palms facing each other over our heads. Finally, as both arms went up, I let go of the barre. In that first lesson we established all of the ballet positions on both sides of the body. Then we moved on to the plie, again in fist position hanging on to the barre with our left hands heels together turning our feet out and open from the hip while maintaining the erect posture with the arched back. The feet moved to the various positions both in releve on demipoint and full plie with the heels down on the floor – every movement was initiated from the lower back into the hip, and the lifted leg was a by-product of the graceful posture – whose tension ended in the pointed tip of the toe. The full set was done first on the right side, then the left side. Several of us had difficulty. The moves were accomplished with us looking straight in to the ceiling-to-floor mirrors both forward and to our side. The teacher moved through our group correcting us as the pianist played graceful Chopin excerpts at the piano. It was difficult for me not to freeze out-right when she corrected my shoulder placement and then the chin for the first time. But I got used to it. The barre lasted half the class, and the remaining time was spent learning slow pique turns and chases which led into the first choreographed dance exercise on the diagonal to the Blue Danube waltz played by our drummer/pianist. We all tried, some of us floundering. The men were the most self-conscious and the rest of us beginners attempted to emulate the best dancers in the class who were exquisite to watch. It was heavenly. Never had my back felt so comfortable, never had I felt more graceful. I thought, "I wonder what would happen to my voice if I sang as I danced."

The class ended too soon. Fridays would be my very favorite day beginning with Bethany's lesson, music theory, music appreciation, vocal practice and then ballet. I fairly floated out the door. I made a note to let my hair grow out. The best ballet dancers had long hair that they placed in a chignon at the back of the neck – a far cry from the modern dancers with the pixie cut that I now sported.

Monday morning I arrived at the music building and descended to the basement to meet Charles Davis, the official Music Librarian. He was a very meticulous man with a modest closely trimmed beard. I took notes as he enumerated my responsibilities. There was a backlog of new arrivals that had been delivered a month earlier. All of them took the better part of a small room. Mercifully there was a standing desk in one corner – but no chair. Since he was backed up, I had to offer a lot of my time between classes during the week and Saturday afternoon. Because of the huge delivery backup, I had to swiftly become the new library expert. There were large books to search the various publishing numbers and each book had a binding on which we placed a stiff strip of heavily glued cloth fabric – color coded to more specific searching divisions, and then another book to look up for the Dewy decimal equivalent which was written in a heavy marker at the top of the spine of the book. There was another set of shelves (already in composer order) that held phonograph recordings of various solo musicians, symphonies, chamber works, orchestral works and opera. If I could not find the original number in the first set of books, I should check the index to the recorded library, and then substitute those numbers to the spine of the book. It was a drudge filled boring job. I vowed my weekend would be spent finding a waitressing job in a restaurant. That paid more, and it would not burn my brain out on trivia that I didn't need to remember in the long term.

Mildly depressed, I escaped to my next class, Honors English. I never thought I would love an English class, but this was like a fresh blast of air once past Mr. Davis. The instructor was a younger collegiate looking woman who wore tweeds and oxford shoes. She insisted we call her by her first name, Elizabeth. Her surname was Weisenfeld. I had been able to buy three of the initial five books. The other two were out of stock, to arrive at the store later. Leaves of Grass, Little Women and Jayne Eyre. However, first Elizabeth distributed a ten page essay, without an author's name, clearly typed on a typewriter, and I thought "what's the deal?"

Elizabeth, taking in the expectant questions written on our faces, laughed. She instructed us to read the entire document, and then we would discuss the content and subtext of the essay. She explained to us that rather than read an entire book to begin with, as a group we would read a shorter document and then discuss it in class. That way within an hour or so, we would have a better sense of what she was looking for in the class content as well as the direction the assignments should written to by us. "Can we mark up the copy in the margins?" Elizabeth responded,

"Yes, that's the point. It will save you time when you begin reading the books, and then organizing any subsequent paper to be written."

Totally intimidated, I began to read, very slowly at first, and then after a page or so, picking up the speed. The essay recounted the first meeting of five individuals, two couples and a solo third, a man named Jerry. Very little description defined the characters. All I could intuit was the tone of their interactions verbally and extrapolate that one couple was American middle class and comfortable, probably man and wife, or simply a paired couple, the other pair were foreigners, the man an Eastern Indian, the woman a Pakistani judging from the description of the clothes they wore and who prepared the other's buffet plate. The final solo person was also American who quickly introduced himself to the hostess and the attendees and then headed directly to the buffet to load his plate up. Ethnic skin color was implied as well as native dress, a flowing pantsuit for the woman and European street dress for the man. Everyone made gentile small talk and circulated. Then the hostess brought a pitcher of wine and made the rounds filling glasses for each attendee from a small liquor cart. Arabian belly dancing music was playing in the background quietly – even then telegraphing the sinuous rhythm. The initial dialog was formal and nearly stilted, and as the evening went on the foreign couple made their way to the paintings on the wall absorbing their colors as they surrendered to the wine .They were very comfortable and happy together. The American couple was less comfortable, and was careful with their wine consumption. They too took in the artwork on the wall, and then sat quietly on the big sofa where the hostess joined them. The lone man, dressed in a good taupe blazer with a white linen shirt tucked into blue jeans, his feet in comfortable moccasin type shoes stayed to himself, and went to the table to load up his plate with food and came away with a diet coke and parked himself in the corner of the sofa away from the other couple. As the ten pages progressed, the story line very slowly began to emerge, but generally left me guessing until the last page. My copy was full of terse notes in the margins. The class collectively had enough of the exercise, some making it through the entire essay, others giving up caught between fear and irritation.

Elizabeth called the exercise finished, and everyone heaved a sigh of relief. "Well, what did you think the purpose of the party was? Why weren't there more people there? Why weren't ethnic backgrounds more clearly stated? Can anyone state clearly what ethnicities were at the party? How do you think the story will end? How long do you think the story should be to arrive at its purpose? What more/societal devices were at play? Were they subtle or did they hit you in the face? Why?

One person raised his hand and ventured an answer. Another person interrupted him and disagreed. What devices did the author use to progress the story? Any ideas of the location of the party? The unique observation was that all variations were acceptable as long as the student could support his observation and find clues in the text to justify it. How conscious of the author and his background and nationality will you be going forward before you read anything? Context is important here.

The class went over to an hour and 45 minutes. The time flew. Finally the teacher wrapped it up, but said, "I'm not insisting you come to anything you read with a bias. I am just insisting that you read thoroughly and comprehensively on the first reading since you will be much more productive in doing so. Can you analyze the various devices the author uses to progress the story?

Now with the above in mind, let's begin by reading half of Jane Eyre and the first third of Leaves of Grass for our next class on Wednesday. Poetry is quite different from prose. Pay attention to authors' literary devices as you read. Make note of them, so we can really discuss this in depth.

I was quite sure that each of us had a blizzard of question marks in our head as we packed up to leave class. Many of us likely felt overwhelmed with the assignment, and a small number of our class likely wondered if Elizabeth was a sadist.

Saturday I arrived at the Annex and took the first hour working vocally. I began with the coloratura albums ambitiously beginning with the Queen of the Night's first aria. The aria begins with a persuasive and cunning cantilena that is meant to persuade Pamina to help the Queen (her mother) kill Sarastro, and then it breaks into dizzying passagework that hangs around the high C and D and passes through the high F above high

C lightly before cadencing beneath. Sometimes that high F just worked. I have no idea how, but it did. Today I got lucky and it worked. Then I began work the slow section carefully making sure the German was accurate and that the breath supported consistently. I got hung up on the "Ach helf" phrase. It didn't feel free. Then I began with Bethany's multiple vowel stream – only slightly better. Then I danced the phrase and it worked to my surprise. I then began from the beginning and vocalized every phrase of the aria with the multiple vowels. Standing still the tongue got stuck somewhere. Moving physically while singing the multiple vowels corrected it. So for the rest of the hour I sang and danced every phrase and alternated standing still with less useful results. Then I sat and played piano and sang simultaneously some Schubert songs. That just sort of worked and the words were clear, but in the fifth directly above middle C the tongue got tighter and tighter until I felt a tight wad of muscle at the base of the tongue going into the neck. Enough. Realizing I was digging a hole for myself I had some definite questions for Bethany on Friday.

I gave up singing and spent the next two hours engrossed in the Brahms Op. 118. Such beautiful music. My piano teacher at Stevens Point had just recommended the G minor Ballade, and discovering the entire Op. 118 was a revelation. So I stumbled my way through it all like a pig bathing in the mud. Two hours went by quickly. I was hoping that I could begin my lesson with Saul on Monday with the A major intermezzo. If ever there was a piece that was an endless melody the A major intermezzo was it. The only thing lovelier to my ear would be the Casta Diva from Norma by Bellini. I finally arrived at the last movement of the Op. 118 based on the plain chant Dies Irae, thicker in texture and more difficult but incredibly powerful and moving. From just the Op. 118 I learned that Brahms fell into my rather big farm girl hands very easily and was a comfortable fit. Then I went to the introductory movement to the Op. 118 which was a big splashy introduction to the set – not as big as the first movement to the Liszt Transcendental Etudes but a similar sweep and bravura. I found I would actually like to perform the complete Op. 118 at some point in the future, if I ever became a really fine pianist.

Saturday, I checked the Madison paper to see if there were any job openings. Somebody suggested I wait a day and check the Sunday paper.

Before that I went through the yellow pages of the phone book. I could tell by the size of the ad which restaurants likely would pay more. I made a few calls, and was asked for recommendations, and I explained that I was looking for part time work, and that I had transferred to the UW Madison that fall. Three people said, "Sorry. We don't train." But out of five cold calls I got two interviews. One at Paisano's, a Pizza restaurant near campus. The other at the Madison Club on the Square near the capital building. I checked out both. Paisano's had a lot of students working, but it did not pay much, so I stalled and told them I would call back Monday. I drove up to the Madison Club on the Square and parked my bicycle. I met two people, one a well dressed head waiter and the other the head chef dressed in white with some red stains on his apron. I found that the job paid minimum wage plus tips – automatic 15% off the gross of the entire bill per customer. That way each waiter/waitress had a more even salary guaranteed on their popularity and work efficiency. I asked them if they did part time on the weekends. They did, and I signed on 5 hours on Saturdays and 4 hours Sunday afternoons. I was told that I would make up the difference on tips since the Madison Club catered to politicians and attorneys. I asked about uniforms, they told me to buy two standard white uniforms, no low necks, washable plus some decent nursing shoes since I would be running a lot. They even recommended the shop that sold them, and please "no hair nets". I wondered how they got past the "hair net" law, but I didn't ask. I just left and biked to the uniform shop.

I began work the next day. I would give my notice to Charles Davis immediately and called into the music library and a voicemail message with the direct number to Mr. Davis replied. He was not very happy with me, and I was told I could pick up my check on Monday for my services so far. I didn't tell him the truth, just said that I found I didn't have the time needed for the work I would have to do for him since I realized now the level of practicing I would have to do.

Sunday morning I left for the Annex again and worked on more Schubert songs as well as the Alte Meister volume. I returned to the Queen of the Night and just vocalized it. The tongue tension was gone. I only had tongue tension when I sang words in the first octave. That was a new discovery. I would ask Bethany about that. Once past the Opus 118, I went straight home to the dorm.

The uniform was dowdy and quite dreadful. The shoes even worse. However the fancy apron that came with the uniform quit nice. I piled on my tight trousers and tank top, stuffed my backpack with my bike chain, the new uniform, apron and shoes, some hair pins and stockings plus a windbreaker and scarf for later and some lip gloss. The commute took me 45 minutes from my dorm. Next time I would come to practice packed for work. And in winter, well I would worry about that when the time came.

At the Madison Club I met with the Chef – that day no hat – just a shock of curly red hair. He explained to me the various work stations in the large kitchen, and where I could help myself to condiments so that I could just take what a table needed with me without asking permission. In 45 minutes I had my section of the dining room stocked. At 4:30 the first customer came through the door. The head water showed him a side table – apparently a personal choice. I noticed that there was a bracket on the wall for the man's outer coat near the table. I had never noticed it before. He waiter told me to finish setting up Mr. Banyon's table. I had finished setting up all the tables in my section, but I learned there was more. Mr. Banyon introduced himself and asked me my name. Before responding to that I asked hm if he wanted a drink or some tea. He ordered a Manhattan and then proceeded to look through the menu carefully. I returned with his drink and he was ready to order: Vichysois, Escargot for the first course, then later two poached eggs with rye toast and jam. I took the order, and as I walked away, I noticed he then proceeded to open a heavy sheaf of papers wrapped in blue. The papers looked official. I went to the cook's station and placed the very odd dinner order immediately. The chef told me Banyon was a unique case. The vishysois had to be boiling hot when placed into the china soup dish, then the dish with the soup in it was placed in the oven to become even hotter. The Chef told me Banyon had eaten the same dinner every day since he had first arrived at the Madison Club. Since the soup was wo hot, I had to bring it on a larger serving plate - all parts of the soup, the container it was in and the silver ware had to be piping hot. So I had a special pair of padded gloves to assist me with this really strange presentation. Even with the gloves on I could tell if my bare skin brushed the plate I would quickly have a second degree burn. I walked back to the Chef's station shaking my head. The Chef and I watched from a distance as Banyon consumed the red-hot soup *without any flinching*. The Chef also told me that as soon as I saw the soup consumed I had to immediately retrieve the empty crockery and return it to the Chef's station, and the Chef would exchange the first course with the second course of two poached eggs and rye toast. I was given the preserves in a small serving cup to take with so the service would be complete on one turnaround. I returned to the Chef's station again and two or three other women had been watching the entire thing and chuckled. Apparently Banyon was used to being waited on hand and foot and they were all pleased to stick me with the job as a mild form of hazing. I was astonished when Banyon gave me the signed check covering the entire dinner with his signature on it plus an additional $20 tip above the standard 15%. The other waitresses thought that if I did well then they wouldn't have to be terrorized by Banyon's quirks!.

The remainder of the evening's service in my section was far less eventful and much more efficient. One of the waitresses said, "Wait until you have to set up a Sunday luncheon with Banyon's cronies. I will show you how to set up the chart so that you get through it without a hitch." 11:00 p.m. came just in the nick of time. I was somewhat tired but not entirely drained. I changed from my uniform in the women's john and emerged as my normal student biker self with a backpack, tight trousers and windbreaker with racing hat and scarf and gloves. The cool air was a welcome change from the Madison Club which was well air conditioned with years of old brandy and extinguished cigar oders lingering vaguely in the dining room.

I unchained my bicycle and buried the bulk weight of the chain beneath my dirty waitress clothes and shoes. 45 minutes later I arrived at my dorm, parked my bicycle near the entrance, locking the chain around the center frame of the bicycle through the front wheel to protect the bicycle from being stolen or disassembled.

The warmth of the dorm was a nice contrast to the now cold outside air. I pulled my clothes off and jumped into a pair of flannel pajamas, went to the john and washed my face and hands from the day's grime. Tomorrow was my first lesson with Saul Carlton. That thought didn't even make me nervous at that hour, and the class before Saul was simply a normal large general physics class which even on an upcoming Monday didn't seem threatening.

I slept like the dead until my alarm clock shattered my dream. It must have been at least a neutral or pleasant dream because I felt excited and positive on getting up. My physics class was in the science building near Bascom Hall. I had all morning to kill before my 4 p.m. lesson with Saul, so I biked out to the Music Annex by 11 a.m. with at least 1 or 2 hours free to practice before I had to return to Music Hall at 4 p.m.

The physics class was just a normal non-honors class to qualify for the science credits for my Bachelor of Applied Music Degree. The woman teaching the class reminded me of any one of my mother's sisters at the age of 55 or so. Short hair, dowdy, pragmatic, and straightforward. Our class easily had over 200 people in it. At a glance none of them looked like brainy geeks. She began the class immediately and directly explaining to us that none of us were going to become an Einstein or anything close to that, however we deserved to be taught something that we would carry forward into our lives once away from academia. She said that the class was geared for intelligent adults who needed to master the basics of physics in a semester and retain enough of the class content to be well-rounded better than middle class citizens who knew little more than how to plug in a toaster. She began by demystifying how to wire a lamp, and what each cord did, what it was connected to, how the connection worked – complete with advanced looking diagrams that would impress anyone I knew. Once past our degrees she wanted to send competent adults out into the world who could function, not be intimated or taken advantage of by handy men who entered our houses to repair things. We were invited to think – even without having read even the first chapter of the heavy book assigned to us for the course. She had our attention immediately, and called for anyone in the class to chime in. If the first student was wrong, she called on another raised hand and gave that person a chance. It was an extraordinary class because each student could put themselves in the position of being a first time apartment renter with a less than well educated super. She got our attention, and she held our attention. Questions were welcomed, students were allowed to brainstorm and enter the fray. The time in the class flew. I felt as though someone had dusted away cobwebs from my brain that had been shut down, but the words "You are a woman. What do you know?" The reply to that inner critic, gave us all the courage to think, "I'll learn". And so we did. That evening I knew I would be reading my physics book, notating my questions in the margin, and that I would retain any notes from the class in my files for future years well after I left college. I later checked out the professor's name at the Science Building. She was the chair of the physics department. Remarkable.

After two hours at the Music Annex, I had read through the Brahms Opus 118 completely – which took less time than before, and then I proceeded to sight read through the first two Beethoven Sonatas from Volume 1 of my Peters edition. I grabbed a sandwich at Rennies and some milk on the way to Music Hall with enough time to use the john and cool my heels for 20 minutes outside of Saul's office.

I heard another student playing as I arrived. And finally the playing stopped. I began to feel sick, and my stomach lurched when Saul opened the door saying, "Next victim." The pianist who was just leaving chuckled. I felt vaguely green at the gills. Saul pointed to the piano bench and I sat down. His studio was cramped and small. Dr. Rupert at Stephens Point had a much larger studio, no less intimidating at the start for me, and finally by the time I left Dr. Rupert I was happy and I had his blessings to become a pianist because I had the talent to and if I *wanted to*.

Saul reminded me vaguely of a huge predatory bird, wings hunched up, beady black eyes, beak projecting well past the breast. Saul's eyes by contrast reminded me of a malicious mischievous imp, the broad smile as threatening as the bird's oversized beak. "What did you bring today?" I replied, "I have been reading through a couple of Beethoven Sonatas and the entire Opus 118 of Brahms". Saul asked for the last movement of the Brahms, and I said, "It's going to be rough." Saul replied,"Just show me what you have and we will work with it." Some sections of it I took up to tempo. Then it became thicker and I had to slow down to get through all of it hands together. "Why don't you practice hands separately?" And I replied, "Because when it's finally assembled you use both hands. Both shoulders have to be reasonably balanced through any practice. Hands alone and I find that my coordination is less balanced from my shoulders into my hips."

Saul thought for a second, and then continued, "Let's take a page at a time. We picked through the first section of it. And in 45 minutes we had gotten through the last movement, with many ideas exchanged. We began the first Beethoven Sonata in F minor. I got through half a page, and Saul interrupted, "Take the artistic pauses out after each of the first two statements of the theme. It's not marked there, and Schnabel years back was looser with his phrasing." And I responded, "But it feels right. It feels appropriate, It's like Beethoven is saying, 'Here's my first idea, no I can do better, here's my second, I am still not happy, ah it's going some place .... Whereto?'"

Saul laughed, Beethoven would have manuscripted that into the music, remember he was a throwback to the classic era." I responded, "So then we have to research back to what some music critic of Beethoven's time said about it before we can proceed and make music through our sensibilities today?" Saul interrupted, "When you have your masters degree and are performing professionally, you earned the right. Do it then. In my studio do only what's written." Five minutes more to get to the end of the lesson and away from his obvious musicianlly monomanic arrogance. We finished. I collected my music and he told me to hold up my hands. I had lost the first digit of my left index finger in a horse racing accident, and he pointed it out and said, "I'm not cutting you any slack for that here." And I shot back, "And I'm not asking for any." Saul's eyes twinkled as I turned and left.

This was going to be an interesting contest of wills. However, his method of practicing the Brahms was a revelation, but Brahms must have had huge hands as I have, unlike Beethoven who clearly had a very agile stretch to the entire hand that allowed for trills in the index finger or middle finger and thumb with quick adjustments to powerful octaves. Brahms was by comparison warm and generous in the hands and heart. Beethoven was rabidly insistent and then elevated with exquisite Chopin-like cantilenas that sang hauntingly.

I escaped and appeared at the Music Library office in the basement. Mr. Davis had already left, and I noticed a very young girl digging through the huge pile of incoming books that I had escaped the week before. She looked tired, she looked beleaguered and I asked if she was a music major, and she confirmed. A freshman applied flute major. She had thick curly red hair, wore no makeup, a partially torn sweatshirt and blue jeans that had seen better days. She was very sweet, and very naïve. She and Davis would work well together. When I asked her about an envelope that Davis had left, she rummaged through the mountain of books in front of her to the back part of the desk and found it. I could sense that she knew some of my background but I filled her in on the voice major with a piano minor for myself and that one weekend of balancing both in practice was enough to make me aware that I could not physically sustain it all. My brain needed rest after classes and all the practice. The last thing I should do was add to it meticulously organizing normal library protocol with musical accuracy and reams of uninteresting abstract applications to something as alive and vital as music. She thought she could manage it with a simple flute major. She wasn't as torn as I was about remaining totally devoted to music.

Long day. Much to think about and very grateful for the waitressing job at the Madison Club. I would never lose touch with "normal people" or so I thought. In time I would find that there were more styles of living than a monastic dedication to music, and that my brain had to somehow straddle it all. I grew up on a farm, and my father would always escape to the fields to work and recover his balance. I was fried, and I had to process Saul's lesson to incorporate that musical expansion into my thought process. So I played hooky and rode my bike to the arboretum. It was further away than I expected, but I found a nice location that was modest in size that jutted out into the water so I could see birds in flight as well as sitting on nests. I walked along the edge of the water and began to unwind. I took out my sketch book that I always carried with me and a felt tip and began to draw, birds in flight, quick strokes, strong strokes and somehow I drew a partial piano keyboard into the mix at the base of the drawing so the birds overhead implied songs on the wing. I began to write at the bottom edge of the drawing and continued .... So much had happened over the week, but so very much potential with so many directions to choose from. After about two paragraphs, I felt calmer and less stressed. I had to admit to myself that I felt guilty that I had left Mr. Davis in the lurch, but I did it immediately so I would upset his immaculate schedule less, and so I could clear my mind completely of the meticulous business of the library. I had to have freedom, distance, physical movement to keep my balance. I began to sing Schubert's Auf dem Wasser zu Singen – singularly appropriate for the location. After which I segued into Michael Head's The Singer. That would always bring me back to my roots, to my family to where my music actually began as a child.

An hour later I jumped back on my bike and 45 minutes later I arrived at the dorm, making a mental note that the arboretum was too far to bike after a late class. The remainder of the week flew with my now filled out academic schedule. Mr. Hetfeld's music theory class was a surreal blur, and I found out a better way of cutting the work down and still getting a passing grade - all the rules and regulations of the forms we studied an odd blur. However the week after I began to feel liberated and not strangled by all the picky details that had been quantified by 20th Century music historians whose espousements filled our music theory textbooks. Hetfeld had told us that each class member would have to compose a short piece "in the style of" various composers we covered in class – an odd take, but who knows, perhaps the application of composing "in the style of" might actually be liberating. Two weeks hence the first lamb would go to slaughter with a number of ad hoc musicians at the music school playing that person's first ever original work. There was one hotshot in class that I could tell most of us disliked. Like any good selection group, when it came turn for someone to raise his hand we all pulled back which left the wunderkind hanging out in the open alone. That was fine with me. If I went later in the semester I would gain from everything I had heard up to that point. Even if I wasn't able to grasp all the rules and regulations of past eras' compositions, I was sure I could invent something credible. And I would wait until the end of the semester to stick my neck out. Hetfeld was aware that I had to work part time, so he might give me a bit more time.

The one really stultifying class was music appreciation. The teacher was in his 60's and rather set in his ways. We listened, took notes, listened some more. And made sure that we could track everything back to Grout's History of Western Music – a very detailed and condensed version of music as most Americans generally thought of it – with only vague references to Alban Berg and Shoenberg which came to the fore just before, during and beyond World War II. To my ear most of the music composed in the 20th Century was abstract like a painting by Jackson Pollack, where Pollack would throw brushfuls of various colors of paint onto a huge canvas working very quickly, allowing it to dry, the next day adding more so visually a Pollack painting reminded me of electrical static that a radio produced when not quite centered on a given station – i.e. the visual equivalent of organized noise. I took meticulous notes so that by the mid-term exams I could refer to them and get through the course without having to read *all of Grout* in the process – a mind-numbing task.

After 90 minutes I escaped from Music Appreciation confident that I had taken good notes concisely so that any exam would take less preparation.

There were two requirements that were big time-wasters. Concert choir and the weekly Convocation. Each applied music student had to perform at least once in Convocation before they graduated with their bachelor's degree. Graduate students were exempt. Each music student in applied had to be part of the big concert choir which met *three times a week (two hours each session!?!!?)* for the first three years of the bachelor's degree. We each had to audition to be placed in the chorus which was typically overloaded with sopranos, very few altos, a couple of actual tenors and the remainder baritones of various descriptions. After one rehearsal I decided (since the high sopranos ALWAYS CARRIED FURTHER THAN ANY OTHER VOICE) that I would lip sinc so as not to damage my vocal technique (as I had when I was in grade school – been there, done that). A lot of wasted time. The Convocations were two hour classes that everyone in the school HAD TO ATTEND weekly. Any musician whose teacher thought them skilled enough, advanced enough and prepared enough, had to perform in Convocation at least once in four years. Bethany had the reputation of holding her students back from the Convocation. They sang once period – and that was it. Sometimes Convocation could be a lot of fun, sometimes some musicians froze under the pressure of their classmates' attendance. Think about it. You work a full semester with a teacher to prepare for a jury exam (voice faculty only), and suddenly without any warning you are in front of 600 plus people – not all of who are interested in singing - without ever rehearsing in the hall. I have seen many people do less than their best in Convocation, where their performances in undergraduate recitals were invariably very good.

The highlight of the Convocation season was Halloween. Saul was the energy behind that particular show. He had every bassoon major, each dressed as a witch with pointed hat, makeup, straw stuck in the hat that streamed all over the floor as they entered the stage carrying their bassoon and playing the main theme from *Sorcerer's Apprentice by Dukas.* Then they stood in a line and performed a reprise of the Dukas to everyone's merriment and cheers. Every Halloween Convocation was HUGE SUCCESS, and very memorable. One year Saul finished with Liszt's

Totentanz which thrilled everyone, and all of the rather jaded students leapt to their feet cheering. He really played the wheels off of it.

During the Christmas season, the older more confident performers would do appropriate excerpts from choruses and operas in chamber with the opera director of the school at the piano. That was a more lofty presentation. However the opera workshop director then finished off the segment with the long involved Anna Russell send-up on Wagner's Ring Cycle playing all the orchestra sections, and singing all the leading vocal parts. He had a rather strong falsetto, and Bruenhilde's Battle Cry was most memorable. The audience was howling with laughter. He really could play. Just a brilliant musician all the way around.

Over all, the high points of my week were my two ballet classes and Bethany on Friday. The remainder of the classes were requirements to be studied, endured and taken with a huge grain of salt to get down. I am obviously a solo artist of a solitary stripe. 80% of my time is spent in preparing, refining and growing. When I perform I look for a sane audience that actually wants to hear what I have to perform, not some requirement to be satisfied with a dose of cod liver oil.

The ballet classes continued in a gratifying steady pace with very clear steady, slow progress. Picking the finest dancer in the class to befriend was important since before class I could ask questions about her training and if I missed something in class she could explain it to me later so I would get it. I splurged on a ballet book of complete positions with diagrams of each dance move (no matter how advanced) which could be broken down and mastered with time. I came in the first day not knowing anything and within a month I was moving well and fit into the class without any particular notice.

On one Wednesday I noticed that the instructor set out three wooden chairs along the wall flanking the door. We all noticed, and then got in line to do the barre. In walked two older women, one a European, grey hair with glasses, they other *my voice teacher Bethany Peterson*! Normally ballet class is where I can learn at an easy pace, improve gradually, *enjoy and be relaxed*. That day stunned my organized world. The instructor introduced them, the European woman had organized the Dalcroze method in Switzerland – a dance system whereby specific arm and leg movements correspond to specific musical beats of a phrase. – beautiful dancing is not the main focus. However moving to the music and filling every note of the phrase with movement and the body tension pulling the dancer through the phrase so there is no flagging or inattention **is**. *Music is in the moment. It can be fleeting. It is sustaining. It is part of the human condition.* Most difficult movements can be broken down to a sequence of activities and the physical transition between the activities to form a complete sustained phrase. It's the equivalent of a singer singing through a long phrase with calm, steady support and each note of the scale of the phrase being precisely lined up and propelled in its own correct time in space. The difference from dance: Singers also have to communicate words and ideas that won't be demonstrated in a physical movement. So the singer has to have all of this going on and stand still quietly and look nice to the audience.

I was excited that Bethany was there, also fearful that I would do something stupid. I got through the class unscathed, and at the end of class the teacher called us aside to talk. Generally he gave notes to the advanced students. He took me aside privately and said, "I know you have never danced before, but you are coordinated and rhythmic. Your body is not correct for ballet – too much bust and shoulders, but learn all the ballet you can here, and when I think you are ready, I will let you know when to move into modern dance. But you really have potential, and it has nothing to do with Bethany. I saw you copy our most advanced student in the first class and you were able to do it all, and this week it's much better so you absorb quickly."

I floated out of class – the best dancer caught up with me and asked, "What was that all about?" And I

told her. She agreed with the teacher since I could do almost any move if I saw it once. She was pleased for me, and relaxed that I wasn't going to become a *grande ballerina?!* Not bloody likely, *but I could quietly dream!*

I was really excited that Bethany had been to my dance class, and that dancing would somehow improve my singing. One more day before I saw Bethany. I flew home on my bicycle and once near the dorm, I walked to the water's edge. It was dusk and I thought, I'm going to practice and vocalize by the water, and see if anything spilled over from the dance class into my voice. I pulled out my pitch pipe. The voice was immediately there. I vocalized accurately to the high E-flat in alt and then began to sing snatches of arias – the two Queen of the Night arias from Magic Flute. The repeated high Fs in the second aria were there. The one high F from the first aria sort of there. So something had carried over from the body into the voice. I rode on my bike a ways, got off and then began to sing again. Every time I stood still for awhile it was less good. Every time I moved or walked it was much better. I realized I had a working solution to certain things that did not quite currently work. I would run it past Bethany.

The next morning I rolled out of bed in a good mood full of anticipation. At that hour I had the shower room all to myself, toweled off and proceeded to dry my hair in the shower room. My roommate was less than understanding at the various hours I was up, and focused more on her general classes and the two boy friends that she currently was involved with. If I had dried my hair in the room there would have been a mildly nasty scene that could potentially negatively set off my day to begin with. I dressed quickly and grabbed some breakfast in the lunch room, stole a second carton of milk and made off to Bethany's office, music and bike chain in my backpack. The air was crisp and damp and I was grateful for the second sweater I had on and the light winter gloves. The trip was uneventful and the traffic thicker than usual. I ended up using my army whistle (hanging from my neck on a lanyard) more than usual. One rather tight call turning on to State Street, but the traffic thinned out as I proceeded eastward.

Bethany was just climbing the steps as I arrived after parking my bike. She hadn't seen me. I waited a couple of minutes until she reached the top of the steps and then made my way up, hitting the landing as I saw her disappear into the john. I followed her into the john, got in the stall just before she emerged from hers. I was hoping to avoid a conversation in the bathroom. With someone of Bethany's background, it would have been terribly awkward, and not a good way to begin a lesson that would likely have far reaching implications for my future. I was excited, and tried not to look as though I was.

We began vocalizing, and this time spent time and detail on body position vocalizing. She was trying something different from last time. And I cooperated. I was a little disappointed that she had not brought up my ballet class. But I noticed that she was using longer passagework this session. Each phrase covered an octave and a half with two passes to the full extension on one breath. I was doing better than the first lesson. But I had been able to vocalize outside on the way home from ballet the night before.

I had made progress on the Abendempfindung which she noticed immediately. Then she mentioned the dance class, and asked how long I had been dancing. I had to admit that I had just 8 months of modern dance at Stephens Point. She seemed surprised. Then she went to her files and retrieved some sheet music, "The Singer" by Michael Head. She told me to learn it and perform it at master class the next Wednesday. She made one further comment which was very telling, "I want you to please choreograph the song and dance it as you sing. So wear something that will allow freedom of movement." I realized that it was a huge sudden assignment for me. She continued, "It was interesting to see you dance. Your body is very elastic and you move consistently through every part of the phrase. It never stops. And the forward tension of that must become part of your singing voice. That's what's missing now. But I am pretty sure you can do it." That's all she said about having seen me in my ballet class. I immediately felt that I I would be in over my head with the assignment, but I like challenges, and this was a particularly creative challenge. She and I read through the song. It was just two pages long but very evocative in F minor. The accompaniment was very simple so the song could be transposed easily in any workable key. The words, some of them at least: "I met a singer on the hill. He wore a tattered coat. His cap was torn. His shoes were worn. And dreamily he spoke, Tra, la, la, la . . . . I met a singer on the hill. My eyes went following after. I thought I heard a fairy flute and the sound of fairy laughter. . . . Tra la, la, la.". It finished with a simply cadenza which gave the song a memorable impression on the first hearing. I was beginning to get a sense of how Bethany's head work, that there would always be a more creative way to do things – that creativity, once discovered, could keep evolving if one just paid attention to the small things. I memorized the song that night, both musically and the words, never realizing at the time that the little song would be with me the rest of my life as an important artistic and vocal touchstone. Thoughts of all of the questions I had planned to ask Bethany were pushed aside. Music theory was predictable, ordinary and onward moving, all very nuts and bolts. Nothing as exciting as the many ideas that were popping into my head so that I could only focus on that song, and how I would want to do it. The song memorized itself and the simple direct poetry became my most referred to thoughts during my waking hours.

Saturday morning came with a new blast of excitement that hadn't been there before. I hired the biggest practice room at the Annex, put on my ballet shoes and began to build physical phrases that matched the poetry of the piece. I began by walking directly down stage on the first phrase, coming to the edge of the stage and presenting much of the first verse as in a direct conversation. I allowed myself all manner of easy turns, using my hands reaching forward to the audience. I allowed myself a tour jete after the words "fairy flute" on the final repeat. Then immediately upon finishing the first phrase of the small cadenza I turned a single pirouette with my right arm overhead and landed cleanly without an off-balance second step, and on the last "Tra la la" I stood quietly looking upward with my arms raised slightly forward. When the last note finished I brought my arms quietly to the sides of my body and looked out to the top portion of the distant wall.

Upon performing it once through after I had the blocking in my head, I noticed that my singing generally had loosened up. The attack was less self-conscious, and I generally made it through the entire phrase on one breath without my previous struggles.

I felt that another rehearsal the day of (which I would somehow squeeze in), and I would perform the piece quite well.

Much of what I had absorbed in my brief rehearsal remained hardwired into my psyche for the rest of the afternoon. I felt as though I was gliding on my feet instead of walking. I worked on the coloratura arias, and they generally went more easily. It was as though a major roadblock that I had lived with for my entire life, suddenly vanished. Then I returned to some

Schubert songs in case Bethany asked for something else. I had no idea who would be playing for me, but if Bethany was running the master class, I trusted that someone would play or Bethany would not have set me on to the quick intense mastery of the Michael Head song.

I realized that it was getting close to 11 a.m. and that I had better get moving to my job at the Madison Club. The afternoon service was light with a few people eating, not politicians. So it was actually very pleasant. And all of them were sober.

That evening Mr. Banyon arrived with his wife and two daughters along with an older married couple who looked vaguely familiar. I didn't immediately place them, and so it took me two hours into the service to realize that I had seen the couple on the cover of the Wisconsin State Journal. They were heavy hitters politically and I couldn't risk any big mistakes. Mr. Banyon introduced me to his guests, "This is my usual waitress. Her name is Edith. And she goes to the university. She's a singer." The couple nodded pleasantly in my direction. Inwardly I thought, "they could care less who I am. Why did he do that?" After I took the drink order, I scurried away to the bar. The bartender jumped right on their order, and I noticed a special milk-based beverage for the two daughters (I surmised that since they were beneath the drinking age that those drinks were non-alcoholic). Mr. Banyon had his usual Manhattan, and his wife had a champagne cocktail. The two guests both had martinis. I always assume that once you begin to drink vodka martinis that you are used to drinking a lot generally. I quietly wondered how gentile the dinner would go if they started that way. But then I also thought that the with the daughters there, everyone would likely be on best behavior. I had served Mr. Banyon before and I never did see him tipsy. But his wife was a blank slate to me.

My memories of the University were fond. The winters there were murder, and the biking in winter very rough, generally replaced by walking bundled up to your eyes. But to this day I call on things that I had learned from Bethany. In four years she made a big impression on me. She was the finest all around musician I had ever met. She was well-read beyond the norm complete with human failings. In retrospect I regret that my timing had not been better. It was well after my move to New York city from Europe that I returned to my notes from Bethany, and her small very worn notebook with illustrations that I had cobbled into place in the margins so I would always have a record. I fell victim to a German singer who took to me. She was with Bethany at the time, and she had raved about her first teacher in Germany, and had her own color coded illustrations in a notebook very much like the one Bethany had given to me. There was that similarity. But Jean felt she knew better about vocal technique that Bethany and she proceeded to take me under her wing and explain how Bethany was wrong about many things. One of my fondest memories of Bethany was when she took me aside in her studio and showed me her scrapbook as a young singer. My she was beautiful, and the photo was a very formally designed image – I thought of Galli-Curci's pics from her time immediately when I saw them. Bethany showed me her reviews, her debut as Queen of the Night in Philadelphia which came early, and then later her marriage to her husband and move to Madison. The University hired her as soon as she began singing recitals and the oratorios of Bach. She got noticed, and remained at the UW, Madison to age 70. She had 10 more years of retirement until she died.

When I went into a vocal crises in NYC after singing the heroic soprano repertoire in Europe after I met Elliot (my lover and best friend of 11 years), I reviewed all of my notes from Bethany. I checked every bit of repertoire she sang, and I realized in retrospect that Bethany was always on the lookout for her students. This control had left me feeling hamstrung and controlled by Bethany. With Jean's influence which was steady and insistent, and the arrival of a younger very glamorous lyric spinto soprano from New York, I switched teachers to the newcomer, and got my masters degree before running off to Europe. By that time I had sung the Ballo Amelia and had been raved in OPERA NEWS, and I had begun to dig into Richard Wagner since my voice had changed a lot. I landed in Europe after my European agent got me into a mess in Bulgaria. Suffice it to say there was no protection in the Eastern block countries those years (and certainly not much now days), and I lost money as well as came home with pneumonia. I found Bulgaria to be a fearful place, much political corruption, and when we were preparing for the concert special, things got precipitously worse. The pollution was thick and grey, the hotel and concert hall a mess (although on TV it photographed better than it was).

Finding a hotel in Sophia tricky – many tips provided with bad service, and lack of security to feel safe in your own room. My audition in Munich got me the connection and my agent made it worse. And my day to day waiting time was spent behind sealed windows looking out over the hotel garbage holding area where neighborhood animals dug through for any food to survive on. I could not believe my eyes when I saw the chicken with her little ones.

Security in
Sophia, Bulgeria
When you sleep.
locked
1 Chair tight against the door
2 Empty glass glass w
metal spoon in it on
the chair
3 Umbrella on door handle
4 Your purse under
your pillow.
→ If someone trys
to break in, there
will be a hell of a
racket & you will
wake up.
Shassel

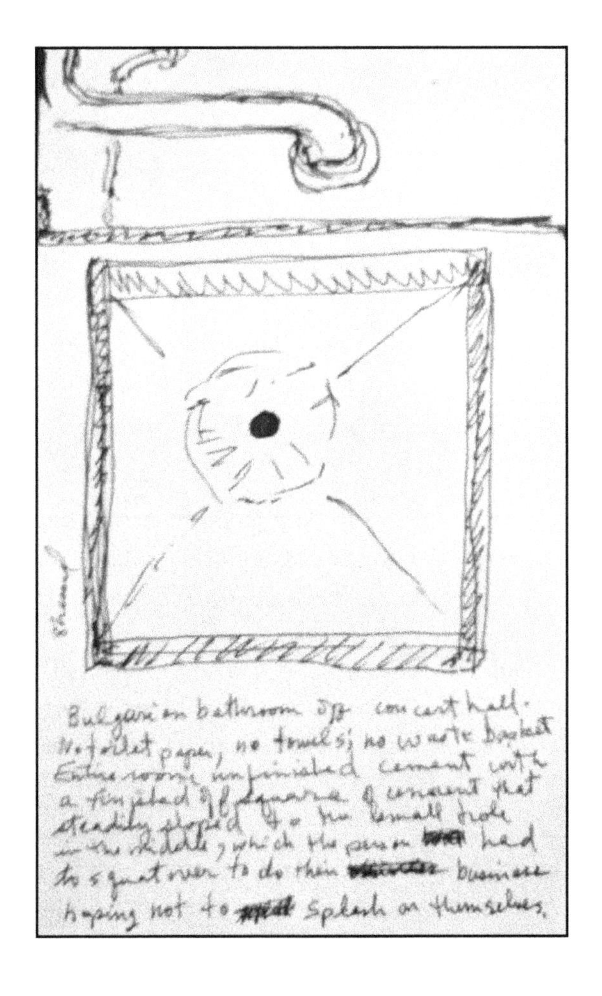
Bulgarian bathroom off concert hall.
No toilet paper, no towels; no waste basket
Entire room unfinished cement with
a finished off square of cement that
steadily sloped to a small hole
in the middle, which the person had
to squat over to do their business
hoping not to splash on themselves.

I returned to New York City and Elliot grateful to be able to find a straight job rather quickly. I vowed never to forget my European stint because my airways could not withstand the constant second hand smoke. Then my beloved Elliot died, and I had to re-invent myself. Elliot loved the Wagner, and I felt that the Wagner had taken a huge toll on my voice, and I set out to find a new way so my voice would hold until I died of natural causes. Once you are a singer, you are always a singer. And my singing is my joy – period.

Subsequently I began to look back to my notes from Bethany's time, and I began to rework the voice at a late age, beginning with the very vocalizes and repertoire that Bethany had taught me. I did not copy the lyric spinto because at the time I thought her technique was faulty. Bethany's voice held really well right into her 70's so she had to be doing something right. Bethany had survived the holocaust and had made her way to South America and then finally settled in Wisconsin. And the more I read about the German coloratura method and traits coming directly from Germany,

Switzerland and Vienna, there was a real way of singing that simply stood the test of time. I treasure my book "How to Sing" by Lilli Lehmann. The margins are covered in markings, and Bethany would refer to that thin volume repeatedly in lessons. That's where I began to rebuild my voice late in life. Without Bethany's insistent "That's right. I know you can do it. You have to put in the work" my voice would have ended years ago. To this day I still recall fondly my time with Bethany. She will always be the chief musical influence for me. Saul and Dr. Rupert are also influencing me today when I play piano and consider new repertoire, but not the profound impact of Bethany. She was unique.

I will never forget my little dance solo in Bethany's master class. I nailed it. I was graceful. All my moves worked smoothly, and the voice poured out of me as it never had before. I had never sung in a hall and at 508 State street, the hall was small, but we still had a stage and a proscenium arch so this was very exciting stuff and each of Bethany's singers, were excellent – all had a coloratura facility – something that I wanted to achieve as well. And I was actually part of the group. I belonged and Bethany was someone to emulate. Every time she demonstrated a phrase in master class, I held my breath. The sound was so lovely, so eloquent, so right. I will never forget her sound. The beauty of that sound moved me to tears – even with just one phrase. Somehow I would have that quality – no matter how long it took me to acquire it.

Pianistically Saul was like a thorn in my side, - a goad – a wise ass – that self-deprecating manner covered up a lot of insecurity. But as I went through the university, I became a crack sight reader because in my free time I always went to the annex and read piano music, and then I would read opera scores, and of course songs. Bethany would criticize me because my fellow students would report back to her that they heard me sing something odd. I would always catch hell for it, and inwardly resented the control she exerted over me.

I made my piano proficiency quickly because I wanted to focus on opera and my voice. So I left Saul in time, but I never stopped playing piano. I never stopped sight reading. Many years later, when I went through my adult vocal crises, my piano playing was there to lessen my fear of how long my voice would hold. And I became a fine piano soloist. You never know who is going to rattle your cage at a young age and inspire you in ways that you could never imagine. I accompanied many recitals at the University, including a complicated chamber affair with a flutist who also played recorder. We had a small chamber orchestra with me at the harpsichord and Julian first flautist. We managed enough rehearsals so that all of the musicians could very nearly breathe together to begin the piece, change sections and cadence without any conductor. Julian was chiefly a conductor-player by choice and love (i.e. a flute major), but by the time we did this big chamber recital, neither of us were studying piano or flute. Julian asked Saul and he sponsored us. Saul attended every recital that I accompanied as long as I was at the University. So I am humbled and grateful for that kind of emotional support - and I had left him as soon as I made my piano proficiency – I only found out how far he had gone to support me many years later. So I will always be eternally grateful to Bethany and Saul. Each of them was simply unique and emotionally generous.

My Evolution as a Pianist and Solo Performer (several articles & program note commentaries):

The below might begin to explain how I finally did become a pianist, and then later a hybrid of that performing as Sue Hassel, Soprano & Piano and later a solo concert pianist. Bethany during one of my voice lessons as an undergraduate told me about a man, a baritone, who toured Germany and Austria as a concert artist singing while playing piano simultaneously the song cycles of Schubert, Schumann and many of the French composers. This suggestion actually stuck in my head over 30 years before it finally germinated.

"Why did I become a pianist? As a pianist I am self-taught. I had four years of preliminary piano as a child. By 4th grade I was accompanying at school for sing-alongs. The children would call out a page number and I would sight-read it. I was an outdoor farm girl who adored horses and did farm chores like any kid who lives on a farm in Wisconsin. At age 9 I lost the first digit of my left index finger tip. During the same year I ran to mount a horse from the side and went over the top breaking my right thumb (only we all thought it was a sprain – so it healed badly). Fast-forward to college: (after 2 years to make my proficiency, I was told to take a double major in piano and voice. Singing was first so I said "no"). I was considered a dramatic soprano, and to save coaching fees I played well enough to learn Ballo in Maschera (raved in OPERA NEWS), Bruenhilde's trilogy, Isolde, Elektra, Salome, Lady Macbeth. By the time Europe called and I began auditioning, I realized that most accompanists did NOT know this repertoire and could NOT play it musically – so I played for myself.

Since my late 40's I have performed as "Sue Hassel, Soprano & Piano", and I have performed two all Liszt recitals and one all Busoni recital – solo piano. Six years ago I began planning for the end of my singing voice (which has not happened yet! – Smile), so I knew I would always play piano for my pleasure and I was lucky enough to be seen by a hand specialist (a miracle worker of a doctor) who finally repaired my right thumb and wrist injury. I had the cast on 13 days. The day it came off I played the first 8 Chopin preludes. To my utter joy the pain was gone. Two years ago I was hit by a bicyclist and dislocated my left little finger. I clicked it back in place as I lay in the street bleeding from my jaw – and the same doctor did an x-ray & some therapy..... it works solidly.

How I plan a piano recital. I am constantly sight-reading for fun, and if I run across something that moves me emotionally I try it out – and in a couple of months I see if it "has legs". "So today's program is the end result of that artistic process pianistically. I gravitate to music with a wide hand-span – and profound artistic contrasts. " (the above paragraph is used frequently as a stand-alone note in my recital programs.)

I was lucky enough to have studied with a tremendous teacher at the Art Student's League who made an enormous impact on the way I do my art – whether it's painting, drawing, writing, playing piano, developing a singing voice or dance. It is all of a piece. It all has a sweep and follow through and an in-the-moment freedom to create something and to allow it to bloom and to trust that it will bloom given enough space and time.

I am most interested in WHY people do things, WHY composers write music, and HOW they go about it, develop and expand through the various stages of their lives. Mussogsky's Pictures grabbed me by throat on the first hearing. Then I read the WHY of how he composed, the descriptions of each movement and the pictures that inspired him to compose the incredible textures and sounds in the iconic musical set.

I love playing piano for the sheer joy of it; for the orchestral colors that I can pull out of the instrument – and the fabulous variety of musical composition that compels me to keep on keeping on. There are varying levels of competence and success among all musicians – including me. What we share with the great masters is the NEED TO CREATE and DEVELOP. It' addictive and it is a life force. SJH

HOW TO DEVELOP SIGHT-READING CAPABILITY AT THE PIANO: - I started piano at age 9, and then lost the first joint of my left index finger in a horse race (yes really!?). I started to play piano two months before the accident and as soon as the splint and bandage came off I resumed playing. My mother would not let me off the hook (I am very glad she was so insistent). Extremely painful – many tears, but the finger became tougher. My sister was the "pianist" in the family. I was the "singer", and I knew if I wanted to learn any repertoire, I had to read better at the piano. Intuitively I knew I was a coloratura soprano, since I could imitate the birds outside. When my sister was out of the house I read at sight her Beethoven sonatas, Schumann Carnival, Brahms Opus 118, and Bach Inventions and Fugues at the piano. I waited until my sister was out of the house, and then I took her current repertoire and began to read at sight. Since I had heard her play the rep, I could tell pretty reasonably how it should sound, and so I persisted. In fourth grade, my classmates called out the hymn number and I played for them at sight (anyone who needs to become a solid sight-reader – reading a four part hymn and any Bach and Beethoven is a good place to start – slowly at first – then in time, up to tempo). Over many years I developed a ferocious sight reading capability, which has saved me money, time, aggravation and bailed me out many times in German and Austrian auditions.

HOW - How to organize playing as one sings. Let's take the Immolation Scene in Goetterdaemmerung. First I straight jacket the entire piece. I sit and sing as I play blocking in the first chord of every measure (I don't have perfect pitch so this means I play my tune with a minimal cord accompaniment below). In this way I have reduced Wagner's structure to a simple hymn. However every interlude gets played completely - no matter how awful the first reading, the harmonic structure is first, then the main tune. Once I have the span of the piece, where it moves in surges, where it is calm, where the big vocal climaxes are, where to save and build the voice to surmount those big climaxes. Since I have a merely competent theory background, my ears have to understand the rest of it, and I have to have quick hands and speedy eye-to-hand coordination to hold it together on a first reading. My eyes are always scanning up and down and then left to right. Over a number of years working this way, you realize each composer has his own formula for composing as his personality. This HOW distillation on sight over years becomes automatic, and the quick coordination becomes automatic, so the most difficult Liszt, Busoni, Richard Strauss, Alban Berg (although with Berg you are dealing with a fixed tone row – forward , inverted and retrograde) and Rachmaninov can be learned rapidly. The standard operatic and song repertoire is child's play by comparison to the more complicated late 19th century to 20th century idioms. I am not diminishing the profundity of the Romantic era composers (this rep across the board is where I live emotionally), but this is how I develop my personal skill set with a very modest musical background. SJH

MY FIRST EXPERIENCE AS SUE HASSEL, SOPRANO & PIANO – As a singer I have auditioned a lot, and even with the standard 19th Century opera rep, I frequently run into pianists who are undertrained, and like me at the age of 9, are thrown into playing for an afternoon of singing auditions. Most usually play Mozart adequately, but they can run into trouble with Verdi and Bel Canto (it's own thing). Rarely are they asked to play Richard Wagner or Richard Strauss. If the singer persists with Wagner or Strauss, the audition can quickly fall apart. This happened to me ALL THE TIME in Europe. I got used to playing for myself the opening Turandot monolog, Invocation from Elektra, Battle Cry, Walkuere (untrained pianists ALWAYS miss the rhythmic return to the A section the second time around!). It takes a determined soprano with huge physical strength and airways of a horse to survive that glitch. And generally they will miss the tempo variations in the Norma Casta Diva Scene (easy to read – BUT treacherous in pacing). In Bulgaria once very early in my European forays I had two different conductors – one Russian (who spoke German and knew his business) and a South American (who had never looked at the Strauss Elektra first monolog). The rehearsal was to get a recording of my operatic excerpts (included Elektra, Turandot, Ring & Norma Casta Diva Scene). I offered to work with the conductor the night before to show him my way with the arias at the piano , but he refused and was offended. Next day, we began with the Elektra in front of his full German speaking orchestra. Three hours later (the conductor did NOT speak German, only Spanish) we got through the first half of the monologue! Every time tempos were wrong, I stopped him by clapping my hands (my agent was freaking out – as was another American conductor in the audience) and then explaining what had to happen in German and demonstrating vocally while conducting myself as to how the tempo should be. The orchestra got it immediately and ignored the conductor and played what I had demonstrated. ***This is a memory emblazoned on my mind!*** **So whenever I auditioned in Europe I MADE SURE I COULD PLAY anything I sang.** You never know what you can run into. ***I always remember that orchestral concerts are collaborations and no matter how stressful, the conductor has to be respected,*** **and with one badly timed down beat, the singer can have a complete fiasco which could prevent him or her from ever singing in Europe or elsewhere professionally!** For the record, after the last take of the Elektra, the German orchestra applauded.

SJH

Another Way to Perform

Over the years, I have presented composite shows (singing a recital group playing for myself, playing a solo piano group & dancing enpointe to my pre-recorded music – show runs an hour roughly. I bring a few of my paintings as the backdrop for scenery – one-time runout). And I also perform in straight recitals as Sue Hassel Soprano & Piano and as a solo pianist, presenting master classes, and listening to many many singers and helping them all (something I really enjoy). I also collaborate with other pianists ad hoc. My finest voice teacher (of all of them) was Bethany Petersen – a coloratura soprano. She told me that before the Nazi's came to power there was a German baritone who toured singing AND playing for himself in Germany the important song cycles. Even as an undergraduate she recommended that I perform as Sue Hassel, Soprano & Piano (my catch phrase for it) since I had the pianistic chops and wherewithal. Her words rang true for me since then to now. ***And so, a lifelong habit, necessity and simplicity of performance has kept me going artistically.***

For the Record - I was always a simple coloratura soprano. I have sung professionally as a Hoch Dramatischer Sopran (Bruenhilde, Elektra, Isolde), Hoher Dramatisch Sopran (Kaiserin, Helene), Verdi Soprano and Dramatic Coloratura Soprano. And because I kept rebalancing my voice with piano, ballet, and much self-recording (Thank you Edirol) as a singer, my voice is still holding. This year I have learned it will only hold as a simple coloratura soprano – and for that I am grateful. That's after two complete cardiac arrests. I am like Secretariat, the race horse, who died suddenly. The necropsy revealed a heart 35% bigger than any other race horse. When they put him out to pasture, he died. So I keep busy and active because my doctor told me that could happen to me. I am a realist, and music is my life. And I thank the audience at the church June 2015 for keeping me alive so I know how to handle my health to keep going. I have a defibrillator in my chest. If my heart stops the machine will restart it – a few times if necessary. I have no blockages, no arrhythmias and I commute by bicycle. SJH

END OF PREVIOUSLY PUBLISHED ARTICLES AND PARTIAL PROGRAM NOTES.

The Art Student's League and Subsequent creative influences (looking back from the vantage point of 2018).

After my brief European career, I stumbled into the Art Student's League in New York City. I had no idea how important that institution was. Thank heaven or I would have been too cowed to attempt going there. I had tried to create a greeting card and had a lot of trouble, so I thought "learn how to draw." So I showed up at their main office, and inquired, "I have never had an art class. I would like to learn how to draw." And the people at the desk said, "Should we put her in Natalie's class? That will be a real eye-opener for her. Or should we place her in a more standard class?" I shrugged my shoulders, and asked, "Is she good?" And they all laughed. "What are the basic supplies?" Mercifully they recommended a few things and the League had a small store of the specific art supplies that were used by the various teachers at the League – and the price point was good.

The next Sunday I showed up to Natalie's class on the second floor at 9 a.m. Roughly 50 other people were in the class – we inhabited a double-sized studio – and we all sat where we were comfortable, each pulling up a small table, if available or a chair that we could brace our pads against the back of. Natalie was in her 30's, very pretty without makeup, dressed loosely comfortable – washed over paint spatters on her jeans with the most incredible shock of pitch black curly hair. Then a female model came in got onto the raised platform in the middle of the classroom and took her clothes off. This was a surprise, but no one else reacted so, 'when in Rome . . .' Initially we drew 10 quick poses in a minute, 5 poses in 20 minutes that were more detailed. Natalie would walk around the class behind each student and peer over his/her shoulders to see how we were coping. She made comments to 4 or 5 students to quickly advise them on how to correct something that didn't quite work. Then we had a five minute break. Then we had four more poses in 30 minutes. That's when I got upset with what I did. Natalie saw that, and made one simple stroke on my drawing and pointed a slightly different way to sit to orient myself to see the model. Amazingly, my drawing improved. We were encouraged at the break to circulate in the space and look at the various drawings each of us had produced so far – so we could learn from each other. I learned in a flash that I drew better than the majority of the people in my class. I seemed to have a facility – and I was encouraged by the discovery. "Perhaps I could become good at this."

The next hour was comprised of two 15 minute poses and one 30 minute pose. I was beginning to get punchy, but I drank a coke and moved to an easel and stood. "That should keep me awake." I faired pretty well with the shorter poses, but during the art class I noticed that what I did came quickly in a rush, and I had no idea how to fill 30 minutes. I asked Natalie about this, and she replied, "You are who you are. If you can do a really detailed drawing in half the time, then do it. But once finished, stand elsewhere and draw the model again from a different vantage point. Each time you draw, it will get easier. Each time you will see differently. Each time it will change. And that's part of the process." I made a mental note to buy a decent fountain pen for the really fast drawings and a small pad, and then buy a really dense dark piece of charcoal to draw the longer poses on newspaper stock – plus a kneadable eraser to shade with. I found the drag on my hand interfered with how fluid my sketching was – and when it was fluid – it was natural and good. In other words, "I had to stop the doubting voices in my head." I remained at the Art Student's League for three years. A year into my classes, I was invited to hang one of my drawings in the gallery during the holidays. I saw after looking carefully at all the drawings and paintings that I was in good company, and that I measured up well enough to warrant progressing further.

Into our second year with Natalie, one Sunday per month was spent on critiquing our work, and we were invited to bring whatever we had ready to show – whether it was done in class or outside. This was really fun and informative because we shared ideas and grew from the exposure. After the first critique one of the more advanced students took me aside and asked if I wanted to show my work, and I of course was interested. So she taught me how to submit photographs of my paintings and I was invited to show two of my works in a gallery near Times Square. The curator was very flexible and imaginative and that began a long term relationship that I became artistically involved in. The curator once said, as I brought one of my canvases to a Flushing location, "Let's show them what a New York artist looks like." And I ended up on Korean television with my paintings. That's what NYC is like. Natalie's influence extended to bringing professional musicians into the Art Students League to perform as the class members drew, painted or water colored at their easels in reaction to what they heard. I performed twice, once with the Turandot monologue, and another time with Elektra's first scene by Richard Strauss – the previous week we had an actress perform the same monologue – the drawings were of a certain quality. After I sang and danced the Elektra, the drawings throughout the class were really wild and out of the norm. I learned by drawing. I learned that the most modest influence a singer/pianist makes can have far-reaching implications. Bethany would have been thrilled with my time at the Art Student's League. And Bethany would have been thrilled at the level to which I became a more than competent modern dancer, and finally a ballet dancer en pointe. Had it not been for my ballet classes in Madison, Wisconsin, had it not been for Bethany's insistence that I dance the songs and arias I sang in Madison, I would have never stumbled into Steps and studied with a world class Russian former soloist at the ABT. That's the point at which I finally became the coloratura soprano that I was born to be – after having survived singing Wagner and Strauss in Europe. Looking back I see that all of the incredible influences shaped me in so very many ways, that to this day I get up in the morning, jump on to my bicycle (rain, snow or sleet), bike to the bridge and vocalize and sing arias for an hour. Yes, the New York Times and the Wall Street Journal have done articles on me "The Soprano on the Bridge", but that's not the reason I did it. I have surmounted two cardiac arrests (due to a genetic fluke in our family) and have a lump of lead in my chest to restart it the next time since it could happen again. My foray to the bridge every day tells me where my body is, how the voice is doing, what I should be focusing on, and how to grow and develop further since I will develop and grow to the day I die.

Looking to the end of life and the Necessary Adjustments to Remain Vital

Years ago, I had planned the order of my artistic decline: Remain physically active as long as you can, i.e. biking, dancing (I still work in professional ballet classes). I am fully aware that's what is holding my voice together at this age. Sing as well as you can as long as you can on your terms. Pick the right repertoire, and record everything so you know *exactly where you are at all times.* When you finally begin to decline vocally, plan your last year recording, include all of the things that you can still sing well and play for yourself simultaneously – that has always been a unique niche I perform in – Bethany turned me on to it many years ago in Madison (i.e. Sue Hassel, Soprano & Piano). When the voice is finally not reliable, play piano publicly in front of audiences (I have become a Liszt/Busoni/Rachmaninoff hot dog type of pianist – great fun, exciting out-there stuff to play – never dull). When I finally have something to say that might be useful to other people in their personal pursuits, begin to write. Spend enough time at it to be a good writer – not just average – push yourself and feel free to bare your soul and connect to other people out there who are pursuing their own dreams, who might be having careers that are lagging, people who without just running across something unique and odd that another creative person might say, could just give up in frustration. Have the generosity of spirit to give unstintingly of your gifts. And when my brain is too far gone to think a coherent thought, return to the Art Student's League and become a dead-earnest painter and watch and learn from everyone at that establishment because that is a great source of creative energy that can transform everyone at any age and of any ability. That forward momentum is organically human. And everyone shares all of their gifts to the ages. I didn't think that I would arrive here at this point in this little book so soon, but here I am, and I think the framing of the above ideas could be premature, but it is organic and unilaterally shared by all people. I have to eternally thank the following influences: My family (i.e. mother, father, sister – all with musical and artistic abilities and naturally beautiful voices and a drive to accomplish), the less than good classmates who bullied me in high school (who made me determined to surmount their destructive influences), Dr. Rupert (who thought I could play piano first), Saul Carlton (who even after I left him, supported me emotionally from behind the scenes for years and enhancing my musical reputation in the process), Bethany (who I left as a graduate student // who to this day is my guiding light for all things alive and musical and vocal – she was the single most creative influence who still guides me from the other side), my Russian ballet teacher (who busted my chops and had me dancing enpointe beginning at age 65!?), Natalie (my art teacher who always said, "Why not?" who allowed me to put all the pieces together and realize the entirety of my personal artistic influences and keep growing), that one English teacher who thought "You really can write if you bothered to revise." And the one very generous published writer in the red coat who took me aside after hearing my very first short story which I had to read out loud in class – which nearly caused a brawl in class, which horrified the teacher. That published writer advised, "You have something special. Don't ever stop." All of these are my influences to push forward on whatever artistic front presents itself next. Each day they inspire me to move forward to see what's just over the next hill. The adventure will never end unless I allow it to fade or die. And that's up to me.

HOW TO KEEP GOING – WHETHER YOU ARE A CREATIVE TYPE – OR SIMPLY AN EVERY DAY JOE. (the less happy life influences)

There is no firm route to proceed especially in our current times when there is so much upheaval. When personally I see so many similarities politically to the rise of the Nazi's in Germany around 1937.

I have found that my years of walking the bridge have allowed me to survive all manner of less than thrilling jobs, of fearful coworkers who create issues that aren't even real; people who are brilliantly gifted; of some unintentional really toxic working conditions. That's a given. In New York City generally speaking we have the smartest, most gifted, well educated individuals – many of whom are immigrants. New York grew to be the best most diverse city because of the immigrants.

I watched a local Facebook town hall type of show last week which included many minorities – all very accomplished people. They were intent on sensitizing each other to the particular problems each of them faced as a result of being a member of a minority race. Each person who spoke had many good points to make. However the gathering and the show came as a result of the multiple pipe bombs that had been mailed to many of the president's critics. That somehow if we could all become sensitized to each other that we could undo the damage that our racist president is implementing daily no different from the incendiary speeches Goebbels and Hitler implemented on their microphones in their mass NAZI rallies which lead to their final solution against the Jews and all the "other than pure German" nationalities present in Austria, Germany and beyond at the time. We have a huge gun lobby that is the equivalent in political strength of the brown shirts and storm troopers of the late 1930's. We have two very wealthy brothers who have bought every representative in the Republican party (they were only able to buy two democrats!). They are so powerful that they can buy elections with tentacles so far reaching that no one in the Midwest is even aware of the influence they are struggling against. And just like the Nazi regime I see the direct influence already in New York City. People are afraid. And they have no knowledge of how big and far reaching the organization is with its various factions. Our president every day bashes the media. Every day in the middle of the night his sick brain writes more tweets that confabulate and deconstruct normal reporting so that both right and left can't really put their fingers *on any source for the news lead* quickly.

My modest creative life does not resonate to people like our president. Check out his background. Our president's father was a member of the Klu Klux Klan. There was an attorney by the name of Cohen who was involved in the Rosenberg case who represented McCarthy who worked on deals with the president's father. These were the childhood influences of our current president. These are the people he looked up to. The liberals in our democracy are being too genteel in their expression of concern. The liberals are generally straight up and very honest and naive. How can a normal person with any integrity counteract the racially motivated life view of someone who has been raised from birth to beat the next guy at all costs – without any consideration of justice or truth - **because the left is** consistently under attack by someone who understands the bully pulpit as Goebels did in 1937, **who doesn't care if he lies** to do it, who gets into an oratorical rhythm in a public speech and engages Midwesterners to chant "lock her up.", who lies about the number of people in his audiences, who lies about everything because he can dominate the dialogue to make a point. Our president realizes that **if you tell a lie loud enough and long enough, it becomes the working truth to the general masses of people who listen**, vote and create divides in society that will destroy an incredible nation like we have now. I have to digress with what is on my mind because my motives as an artistic and creative person are quite pure and devoid of politics, but when stormtroopers came to the doors of the European middle class, ***they couldn't hide in the music of Chopin or the sensibilities of Monet and Renoir***. You have to survive to be able to enjoy artistic pursuits, to create, to even think creatively.

The Midwest is completely hoodwinked by our president. New York is not. However New York is naïve enough generally to believe that if people remain civilized they can persuade other similar people to turn the tide against the president's nationalist agenda. However, there are people who don't earn a lot of money, who don't know how to play the market, who survive and live in blue collar midwestern locations on blue collar salaries. **They are now the majority**. How does one continue to create with the above going on in our country? How can one create in good conscience when the threat of losing everything America has become since its inception **is at risk**?

The Nationalist agenda can destroy us if too many of us are complacent with our assumed liberal status and serenity. Everything that stabilizes a humane society is at risk. How are we creative during this time? How can we create without feeling guilty?

Millions were killed by the Nazis, but the society of the educated classes, with solid religious history did sustain through the time – many of their number decimated. I won't enumerate how many of the most important religions were involved with the Nazis at the time, but there were many. That's what we have at risk right now in America.

And just now the New York City news is crowded with coverage of the shootings in the Jewish Synagogue in Pennsylvania. Twelve people dead because of someone who heeded our president's rhetoric. Some who perished had survived the first holocaust in Germany, and thought they were safe, thought that "America was different and free from terrorism."

So perhaps going forward, I will recover from the queasy feeling in my gut, push through the noisy static, incorporate the influences of the toxic rhetoric–and finally come out the other side with some type of emotional balance that I can live with, that has some integrity. **I will search for the way forward. Each of us needs to search for his own way forward**.

CPSIA information can be obtained
at www.ICGtesting.com
Printed in the USA
LVHW041219210820
663783LV00005B/296

9 781647 490652